LIFE
UNLEASHING *the* POWER

WIDE
of a PASSIONATE LIFE

OPEN

LIFE

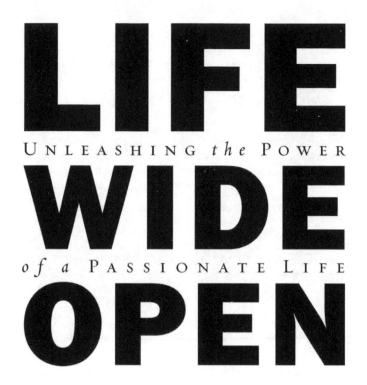

UNLEASHING *the* POWER

WIDE

of a PASSIONATE LIFE

OPEN

DAVID
JEREMIAH

Author of the Bestseller MY HEART'S DESIRE

INTEGRITY
PUBLISHERS®

Nashville

Copyright © 2003 by David Jeremiah.

Published by Integrity Publishers, a division of Integrity Media, Inc., 5250 Virginia Way, Suite 110, Brentwood, TN 37027.

HELPING PEOPLE WORLDWIDE EXPERIENCE *the* MANIFEST PRESENCE *of* GOD.

Published in association with Yates & Yates, LLP, Literary Agents, Orange, California.

Unless otherwise indicated, Scripture quotations are taken from The New King James Version, copyright © 1970, 1980, 1982, Thomas Nelson, Inc., Publishers. Used by permission.

Other Scripture quotations are taken from the following sources:

The Holy Bible, New International Version, copyright © 1973, 1978, 1984, International Bible Society. Used by permission of Zondervan Bible Publishers.

The Message (MSG), copyright © 1993. Used by permission of NavPress Publishing Group.

The New English Bible, copyright © 1961, 1970 by the Delegates of the Oxford University Press and the Syndics of the Cambridge University Press, 1961, 1970. Reprinted by permission.

Cover Design: Bill Chiaravalle
      www.officeofbc.com

Interior: Inside Out Design & Typesetting

Library of Congress Cataloging-in-Publication Data

Jeremiah, David.
Life wide open : unleashing the power of a passionate life / David Jeremiah.
p. cm.

ISBN 1-59145-065-9 (hardcover)
ISBN 1-59145-120-5 (international paperback)

1. Christian life. I. Title.
BV4501.3.J465   2003
248.4–dc22   2003017228

Printed in the United States of America
03 04 05 06 07 BVG 9 8 7 6 5 4 3

To my wife, Donna

For forty years

we have shared

LIFE WIDE OPEN

LIFE WIDE OPEN

UNLEASHING *the* POWER *of a* PASSIONATE LIFE

Contents

Acknowledgments

JOEY PAUL AND BYRON WILLIAMSON of Integrity Publishers believed in this book from the first moment we discussed it. Joey, your notes, e-mails, and creative ideas kept me going!

Sealy Yates, of Yates and Yates, is my literary agent and most of all, my friend. We have worked together for over ten years on more than ten books. Sealy, I can't imagine writing without your counsel and encouragement.

Rob Suggs understands my heart. As my editor, he organizes my words and makes them come alive. Thank you, Rob, for your passionate work on *Life Wide Open!*

This is the third project Jennifer Stair has coordinated for Integrity Publishers. It is such a delight to work with you, Jennifer.

Paul Joiner, Rob Morgan, William Kruidenier, and Ed Stewart read this manuscript and offered valuable suggestions and assistance. Thank you, men, for helping me pull all of this material together. I am grateful for your contribution to *Life Wide Open!*

Helen Barnhart managed this project from my office. When I was on the road, she e-mailed and faxed me material so that I could stay on schedule. Helen, your humble work behind the scenes enabled me to do what I do. Thank you!

Carrie Mayer schedules my days and manages my office. Carrie, no one would believe all that you do in one day. I am continually blessed by your efficiency and your effectiveness.

Barbara Boucher works tirelessly as my personal secretary. Hundreds of demands that are part of a large, growing church never reach my desk because she handles them with wisdom and class. Barbara, I am honored to be represented by you at Shadow Mountain Community Church.

My greatest asset is my wife. From the very beginning, she has been a quiet, behind-the-scenes partner in all that God has given me to do. Donna, the inspiration of your faithful support becomes more important to me with each passing year.

I want to acknowledge two men who administrate the ministries that I have been leading for the past twenty years. Dr. Tom Thompson is the executive pastor of Shadow Mountain Community Church. Thanks, Tom, for managing the details so that I can concentrate on the main thing God has called me to do.

David Michael Jeremiah is my oldest son and the director of operations at the international ministry of Turning Point. During the time I was working on this project, David was managing the construction of a new headquarters building along with his many other responsibilities. David, I am so grateful for your love for Jesus Christ and your commitment to serve Him at Turning Point.

Most of all, I want to thank God for calling me into ministry. The story of His leading in my life is at the center of this book. As I review His gracious dealings with me, I am filled with wonder and awe. I continue to learn that only the life that is lived for Him is "life wide open."

—DAVID JEREMIAH
San Diego, California
July 2003

Introduction: Open Wide!

EVERYWHERE YOU GO, YOU MEET THEM—the ones who sit on the back row of life, whisper, and roll their eyes. These are people who aren't really headed anywhere, and they're eager to criticize those who are.

Today, we call them cynics. In Jesus's day, they were called Pharisees.

I don't know what they were called in the early days of this country, but I know that even then they were around. There is a story of Benjamin Franklin speaking to a crowd on the wonderful guarantees of liberty provided by the United States Constitution. Midway through his talk, one of these cynics called out, "But what about this 'pursuit of happiness'? Where's our guarantee of happiness?"

Franklin smiled and replied, "My friend, the Constitution only guarantees the American people the right to pursue happiness; you have to catch it yourself."[1]

By now I believe you've discovered Franklin's observation to be true. Happiness is no entitlement. There's no government funding for it. You can't buy it at the health-food shop or the ritziest store in the mall. Contrary to popular opinion, wealth isn't even a distant relative of happiness.

Yet there seem to be a lot of people in this world who are

puzzled about where exactly the bluebird of happiness makes her nest, because all around us are passionless lives, lives idling in neutral, and lives out of focus. Deep down in our soul, we feel that we should be able to live life *wide open*. From a distance we have caught sight of this exotic quality called *passion,* exhibited by certain characters from books or in the movies and, every so often, someone we meet in the real world. These are people who "grab for the gusto," as the old television commercial used to say.

What is their secret? How does one go about "grabbing for gusto"? A small handful among us have discovered what the rest of us would pay dearly to know: How can we bring real, living *excitement* into this life? Not some cheap, store-bought, amusement park-simulated excitement—we mean the genuine article. What is there that could possibly make us eager to leap out of bed in the morning, filled with laser-intense purpose, exhilarated about the prospect of another twenty-four hours on earth?

We'd really like to know, because many of us are not living a life wide open—not by a long stretch. We're closed shut. We are passion-impaired, though we have surpluses of longing, yearning, hopelessness, loneliness, and purposelessness. We can remember the times when our blood was really pumping, when our heart was skipping beats, and when it seemed there was some purpose we were reaching toward with everything in us.

This book is a map to the life of passion and purpose, the life wide open, based on the best wisdom we've been able to glean from the Word of God these two thousand years. About that long-ago time lived a man known as Jesus of Nazareth, and we believe He held the key to ultimate power for living—more precisely, we believe He was the key.

As I've assembled this book, I really believe I've included some truths from the heart of our Lord that will totally transform the way you see your existence and your purpose. I'm hoping that you won't read these pages the way you read most volumes—from a kind of rational distance. I hope you'll read it reflectively, pencil in hand, with a spirit of candor—wide open.

Introduction: Open Wide!

I pray that you'll ask yourself some hard questions, and that this book will help provide the answers as they relate to your life. As that happens, you won't have to wait to see tremendous changes occur. Your life can begin its transformation tomorrow, today, *right now.*

The Spirit of God has not set a goal that you would get it all together ten years, or even two weeks, from now. He is raring to go! He is in a hurry to help you get to the good things that lie in wait for every human being on this earth. He stands now on the outskirts of your soul, helping you read this page and applying its ideas to your life as He whispers, "Yes! Read it closely! This is where we're going!" Can you hear His voice? Can you feel the changes that are rolling in like a spring rain?

As we depart on this journey toward the life wide open, my prayer is that you begin by opening wide! Open your heart. Open your mind. Then open your daily calendar and set a course of adventure through the daily rounds of your life. This is the *passionate* journey—the quest for all the deepest riches of living in the presence of a God who absolutely, unconditionally, passionately, and wide-open adores you.

Open wide! Here comes the first course.

1

LIFE
UNLEASHING *the* POWER
WIDE
of a PASSIONATE LIFE
OPEN

Pedal-to-the-Metal Living

IN A SMALL TOWN IN KANSAS you will find what is certainly one of the world's largest balls of twine. You know, of course, that I would never lie to you.

At last count, this ball of twine weighed nearly nine tons. It is a full forty feet in circumference and would stretch nearly fifteen hundred miles long—about halfway across America, in case you're interested in testing it out. The originator of this ball of twine started his work in 1953, but he died just before he reached his goal of having the world's largest one. Today, the whole town pitches in to keep the ball of twine growing.

At this point you may be tempted to take a deep breath and say, "Well, that's . . . *unique!*" But you would be wrong. A town in Minnesota has what they declare to be the *true* world's largest ball of twine, weighing in heavier than nine tons. And there are several other towns racing to be recognized in the *Guinness Book of World Records* for their own monster twine balls.

Whatever else you may say about such a pursuit, you have to be impressed by the passion of those who focus the great energies of their life on one very precise goal. What is it inside a man, a woman, or a town that would drive them to spend all their spare moments for fifty years accumulating a ball of twine? Or building a replica of the Eiffel Tower out of toothpicks?

For that matter, if we are really honest, what keeps you getting out of bed each morning, facing an untidy house or a stressful business career? You might say, "That's an entirely different matter! We're not talking about a hobby. I have to make those beds and wash those dishes or our home will be in chaos. I have to put in a productive day at work or the checks will stop rolling in. I do what I must—out of sheer necessity."

There we have it. You do what you *have* to do, not from passion but from obligation. There's a world of difference, isn't there?

Yet it wasn't always so. Can you remember the first morning in your home, when the boxes were still packed? Can you think back to your first week on the job, before your business cards were even printed? Perhaps there was a little something more that moved you forward then. Perhaps there was excitement and energy, and you were *impassioned*. The time flew by as you went about your work, for this was a new life. This was the goal you had been aiming for. There were new areas to explore and new facts to discover about yourself.

Marriages begin with passion. We believe the honeymoon will last forever.

Faith begins with passion. We believe we'll live on a spiritual mountaintop forever.

For that matter, you may experience passion—of a sort—for an object: a new wide-screen television or a luxury automobile with that new-car smell. It may not last long, but if one man can be passionate about a ball of twine, you can certainly be excited about your car!

The question is, Why does this intense dedication wear off? Why does the thrill fade like a T-shirt image after a few rounds in the washing machine, like a peeling bumper sticker or sun-bleached wall poster?

Why can't we live with passion every day of our life? If we could package passion in a can, we could make millions of dollars. If we could use it every day, then this life would bear more than a passing resemblance to the next one.

I am absolutely convinced that life is meant to be lived with powerful emotions and heightened expectation—with joy, fulfillment, excitement, and purpose. I am convinced that when we live with passion we honor God powerfully, for it is then that we resemble Him most in spirit. He created us *passionately,* with joy and commitment to us, and His love for us has never worn off.

I'm not talking about the passing fancy du jour. I'm referring to something that penetrates deeper than the emblem on your shirt and a philosophy too complex for a bumper sticker. I'm referring to a kind of life that doesn't eliminate the occasional blue Monday but powerfully transcends it. Passion is all about a basic mind-set and a heart attitude for embracing life—positively, energetically, full bore, pedal to the metal, wide open.

I think the passionate life is what Jesus was talking about when He promised, "I have come that they may have life, and that they may have it more abundantly" (John 10:10). It's the "first love" described by John in Revelation 2:4—a "first love" that is not designed to wear off.

RUNNING WITH PASSION

Instead of dissecting passion as if it were a laboratory specimen, I'd rather show you a picture of what I mean. The Scottish Olympic gold medalist Eric Liddell is a compelling picture of passion. He was immortalized in the 1981 Oscar-winning film *Chariots of Fire.* Liddell, portrayed by the late British actor Ian Charleson, was born in 1902 to missionary parents in China. While his father, mother, and sister ministered in China, Liddell and his brother attended boarding school in England and then the University of Edinburgh. It was at the university that his athletic prowess attracted the attention of his countrymen.

Apparently Liddell's godly missionary parents encouraged their son's athletic endeavors. In the movie, Eric, his father, and his brother are discussing the topic during the parents' furlough in Scotland. The elder Liddell says, "Eric, you can praise the Lord by peeling a spud if you peel it to perfection. Don't compromise. Compromise is a language of the devil. Run in God's name, and let the world stand back in wonder."

Chariots of Fire tells the dramatic story of Liddell's rise to prominence as a sprinter in Great Britain, culminating in victory in the 1924 Olympics in Paris. His gold medal in the 400-meter dash and a bronze in the 200 confirmed his title, "The Flying Scot."

Eric Liddell was deeply passionate about running. But he had another deep passion. As the movie portrays, he loved God even more than he loved running. Liddell took advantage of his popularity to speak to crowds about his love for God. In one scene of the movie, Liddell compares life to a race, concluding, "If you commit yourself to the love of Christ, then that is how you run a straight race." After his triumph in the Olympics, Eric Liddell returned to China as a missionary and served God passionately until his premature death from a brain tumor at age forty-three.

Liddell saw no conflict between his two great passions. It was impossible for him to separate his passion for running from his passion for God, because he knew that both came from the same source. His sister worried that athletics would rob him of his fervor for God. But Liddell told her, "I believe that God made me for a purpose: for China. But He also made me *fast!* When I run, I feel His pleasure. . . . It's not just fun; to win is to honor *Him.*" Liddell had tapped into a vital truth in the Bible: "Those who honor me I will honor" (1 Samuel 2:30).

The Flying Scot did not regard running as an opportunity to glorify himself but as an opportunity to glorify God, the source of his talent. To run without passion would have tarnished the passion he professed for God. He believed that his athletic ability was to be managed and used for the glory of God. Therefore, as a servant of

God, he honed and utilized his gift of speed in a manner that would please his Master, the Giver of his gift. And he did the same as a missionary in China.

THE PASSION PRINCIPLE

Eric Liddell unlocked the secret to the passionate life. His life stood as a model of the "passion principle" described by Paul: "Whatever you do, do it heartily, as to the Lord and not to men, knowing that from the Lord you will receive the reward of the inheritance; for you serve the Lord Christ" (Colossians 3:23–24). During Eric Liddell's university years, "whatever you do" centered on running. Afterward, his life focused on missionary work in China. And he did them both "heartily"—flat out, wide open, passionately—"as to the Lord." The passion principle directs us to approach all our activities—indeed, all of life—the same way.

A fulfilling, passionate life comes from the inside out. Many of us sense that something vital is missing in our life. By society's standards, we may already be considered successful. We never go hungry; all our needs are met; we have our friends and our family. But something is missing, and deep in our soul is a stubborn insistence that *there must be more* to life.

We want to find that "more." To begin with, we want a faith in God that is vibrant and alive. We want to make a difference in our world. We want *more* in our jobs, *more* in our homes, *more* in every relationship. We reach out for a life that crackles with hope, enthusiasm, energy, and anticipation. And we hope beyond hope that we can wrap our fingers around it and claim it as our own so that we might experience a life wide open.

Jack London eloquently described this kind of life: "I would rather be ashes than dust! I would rather that my spark should burn out in a brilliant blaze than it should be stifled by dry rot. I would rather be a superb meteor, every atom of me in magnificent glow, than a sleepy and permanent planet. The proper function of man is to live, not to exist. I shall not waste my days in trying to prolong them. I shall use my time."[1]

Put that on your bumper sticker! Surely every member of the human race would stand to affirm his or her desire to have and to hold the thing London describes. But something is holding us back—could it be our fear?

Yes, we must admit it: We are afraid.

We're afraid that life wide open will be *too* wide open. It may streak into the sky like a comet, beyond our control, outside our comfort zone. We want to be passionate, but we don't want to appear insane! We want to plunge in, but we don't want to drown.

So there we stand, glued to the dock, gazing wistfully at the water and dipping in a toe every now and then, imagining what it must be like to swim. Something, we know, has to happen. It's called the leap of faith, and there's no such thing as a halfway leap. At some point we have to leave the ground, soar into the sky, and give ourselves to the living waters of God's boundless provision.

Will you trust God to be waiting for you, hands outstretched? Are you willing to move forward into the thrill of His future without a backward glance to the drudgery of the past? Jesus spoke of taking your hand off the plow and following—*now*—wherever He leads (see Luke 9:62). To find the passion you seek, you must be passionate about seeking.

I believe you have that seeker heart. Something vitally important is missing at the core of your soul, and, despite the apprehension you feel, you are ready to go for it. Don't be like the anonymous writer who came to this realization too late:

First I was dying to finish high school and start college.
And then I was dying to finish college and start working.
And then I was dying to marry and have children.
And then I was dying for my children to grow old enough so I could return to work.

And then I was dying to retire.

And now, I am dying . . . and suddenly realize *I forgot to live.*

Take a look at one more bumper sticker. This one is imprinted with the words *Carpe diem.* Those Latin words signify "Seize the day." That's what we call an imperative with a strong verb: *Seize it!* The phrase implies immediacy. The day, after all, is as fleeting as the deer in the woods. One moment of hesitation and it's gone forever.

Seize the day by seeking its Maker. Revise the bumper sticker slightly, to read *Carpe Deum:* "Seize God"—and don't let go! If you have never reached for His powerful hand before, you're in for a great adventure. He alone is the source of true passion for all you do in life.

Part I

Get a Grip on the Passionate Life

HAVE YOU EVER WATCHED A ROCK CLIMBER? Now there's a person who commands my respect. He stands at the bottom of some fabulous and forbidding canyon, a scar cut deeply into the face of the earth in the course of thousands of years. He lets his eyes wander upward, shielding them from the sun as he glances at the summit—his goal.

How will he ever get to there from here? What kind of person would risk the dangers of such a climb? He may be sixty or seventy feet in the air before that moment comes—the moment when his grip is less than sure, the moment when his fingers grope for a crevice and come up with nothing but air and unforgiving stone, the moment when nothing but his quick wit will keep him from toppling to his death far below. He risks all this for passion, for the thrill of standing on the top and knowing he has proven worthy of the task.

We stand transfixed as we watch the rock climber because we know that we are seeing something more than the sporting life at its best. We are beholding a microcosm of the long, hard climb of life itself. All the elements are there: beginning at the very bottom; setting our sights on the summit; the blood, sweat, and tears that lie between; and the careful climb, step by methodical step, with its moments of exhilaration and instances of sheer terror or fatigue.

You and I stand right now and gaze toward the top. We mean business. We know we want to arrive at the place where life is all that it was meant to be, the place our soul tells us is real, where the wind is cool and the view is infinite. We are eager to begin the climb, but we need to *get a grip*. We look toward that first place where our chisel will ring as it cuts into the stone, allowing us to pull ourselves up, if only a few feet. It's a humble beginning, but it's a start.

Think of these next few chapters as your climbing instruments: your chisel, your backpack, your steady resolve. If we're going to make it all the way to the top, we need the security of knowing we're reaching for solid direction and standing in footholds that will not give way.

Let's take a deep breath, gather our resources, and begin that climb toward a life wide open.

2

LIFE
UNLEASHING *the* POWER
WIDE
of a PASSIONATE LIFE
OPEN

Give Everything Your All

L ANCE ARMSTRONG has won Le Tour de France, the world's most prestigious bicycle race, an incredible five times in a row (1999–2003), becoming the second person ever to accomplish such a feat. He has already announced his plans to compete again in 2004. For one individual to dominate a sport in the way of an Armstrong or a Michael Jordan would be achievement enough for nearly any life. What makes Lance Armstrong's story remarkable is that he was fighting cancer as late as 1997.

It was passion for life that saw him through the cancer and passion for racing that made him a cycling champion. Listen to the energy that crackles in his words:

I want to die at 100 years old with an American flag on my back and the star of Texas on my helmet, after screaming down an Alpine descent on a bicycle at 70 miles per hour. I want to cross one last finish line as my . . . wife and my ten children applaud, and then I want to lie down in a field of those famous French sunflowers and gracefully expire, the perfect contradiction to my once-anticipated poignant early demise.

A slow death is not for me. I don't do anything slow, not even breathe. I do everything at a fast cadence: eat fast, sleep fast. It

11

makes me crazy when my wife, Kristin, drives our car, because she brakes at all the yellow caution lights while I squirm impatiently in the passenger seat.[1]

Lance Armstrong is a man who knows how to live. He understands that the greatest enemy is not death but a life unlived. So he has set out to live a life wide open as he races through the sunlight of the wide-open outdoors, wind in his face and joy in his heart. He shares that same kind of passion with Keefy, whose story is told in Mike Nappa's book *The Courage to Be Christian.*

Keefy spent his boyhood as a fan of the Minnesota Vikings. He was no more than a small child in a Hartford, Connecticut, ghetto—or was he, in fact, more than that? In his imagination he was Chuck Foreman, the Vikings' slashing running back. He may have played in dark, littered streets, but in his mind's eye they were an emerald gridiron.

Keefy spent every possible hour playing football in those mean streets of Hartford. He kept before him the image of excellence in the person of Chuck Foreman, whom he studied carefully on game telecasts. Emerging into the alleyway again, he would copy the moves he had seen—spinning to avoid a tackler here, lowering his head to bowl over a defensive back there, starting and stopping on a dime. Keefy understood the beauty and the brilliance of an all-pro running back.

Keefy and his brother were playing ball with the neighborhood crowd one day when Keefy was sprinting out for a deep pass. His brother, the quarterback, released a long bomb, and Keefy strained every molecule of his body toward the goal of running under the pass. By all reckoning the pass was overthrown. But Keefy kept running then lunged and leaped. At the last possible second he took flight and saw the ball settle perfectly into his taut fingers—and he paid the price.

Keefy crash-landed onto the pavement and scraped his face on the gravel. But just as quickly, he was up and beaming. "Did you see that catch?" he called out. "It looked just like Chuck Foreman, didn't it?" His friends, wide-eyed in amazement, began to chant his name. He felt like the king of the world as he lifted the ball in triumph. But as he approached his friends, their faces grew somber. Finally one of them said, "Man, look at your ear!"

Blood was seeping down Keefy's shirt from his deeply torn ear. He had nearly severed his ear from his head but hadn't even noticed in the passion and joy of his pursuit.

That passion and joy carried him all the way to the NFL, in the footsteps of Chuck Foreman, and to the Pro Bowl on several occasions. That passion was an integral element when Keefy helped the Green Bay Packers win a Super Bowl. Keefy, better known as Eugene Keefe Robinson, has made his share of mistakes, to be sure. Some have been very big and very public. But his example of passionate commitment to the game of football is second to none.[2]

WHATEVER IS WHATEVER?

Genuine passion swells to take in *all* of life—the total package, the whole enchilada. The passion principle in Colossians 3:23–24 calls us to do "whatever we do" heartily, in a way that Lance Armstrong and Keefy Robinson would understand: "And whatever you do, do it heartily, as to the Lord and not to men, knowing that from the Lord you will receive the reward of the inheritance; for you serve the Lord Christ."

There's no mystery to the word *whatever*; it simply refers to every task we undertake. But let's take a few moments to unpack *whatever* just to make sure we understand what's included.

1. Whatever *includes anything you must do.* We're talking about your duties and responsibilities as a citizen, a spouse, a parent, a child, an employer or employee, and so on. In the verses immediately before Colossians 3:23, Paul specifically addresses these roles and their principal obligations:

13

- "Wives, submit to your own husbands, as is fitting in the Lord" (v. 18).

- "Husbands, love your wives and do not be bitter toward them" (v. 19).

- "Children, obey your parents in all things, for this is pleasing to the Lord" (v. 20).

- "Fathers, do not provoke your children, lest they become discouraged" (v. 21).

- "Bondservants, obey in all things your masters according to the flesh, not with eyeservice, as men-pleasers, but in sincerity of heart, pleasing God" (v. 22).

Notice that Paul makes no distinction between pleasant and unpleasant duties. We are to dive into all our tasks passionately and enthusiastically, including such challenges as fixing a leaky faucet, changing diapers, paying the bills, resolving a conflict with our spouse, filling out a tax return, etc. Borrowing the motto of the United States Army from a few years back, "Be all you can be" in whatever job you must do.

2. Whatever *includes anything you choose to do*. What happens when you're not "on the clock" at work, at school, or at home? It's free time and you can do whatever you want. Maybe it's playing golf, making crafts, traveling, wrestling with the grandchildren, sewing, taking in a ball game, going for a walk, or playing a computer game. Jump into your leisure activities wholeheartedly and with enjoyment. If you are paralyzed with guilt over having a good time—even when you deserve and need some R&R—you're not living passionately.

3. Whatever *includes anything you are gifted to do*. Eric Liddell knew that God made him for ministry to China. He hastened to add, "But He also made me fast! When I run, I feel His pleasure."

In what area has God made you "fast"? What are your unique talents, gifts, and skills? Bud Paxon put it this way:

God has uniquely wired each one of us to possess special desires and aptitudes. The vision you have for your life, family, and career can be expressions of your God-given passion. Take the time to routinely pray and daydream about what you would be doing if you could have your cake and eat it too. What would your life look like if you were doing what you wanted to do? What would you be doing if you implemented your dream? Keep in mind to daydream with God at your side.[3]

4. Whatever *includes anything you are commanded to do by God.* I'm thinking about two sweeping directives in the Bible that apply to all people at all times: the Great Commandment (see Matthew 22:36–40) and the Great Commission (see Matthew 28:18–20). We are commanded to love God and people and to teach others to do the same. These basics are at the epicenter of God's passionate desire for our life. So we are very wise to become passionate about those things that spark God's passion.

It is easy to become overwhelmed by the vastness of God's mission for us. We must remember that anything God wants us to do begins within us. An unknown monk writing around A.D. 1100 recorded these words:

> When I was a young man, I wanted to change the world. I found it was difficult to change the world, so I tried to change my nation. When I found I couldn't change the nation, I began to focus on my town. I couldn't change the town, and as an older man, I tried to change my family. Now, as an old man, I realize the only thing I can change is myself, and suddenly I realize that if long ago I had changed myself, I could have made an impact on my family. My family and I could have made an impact on our town. Their impact could have changed the nation and I could indeed have changed the world.

What this monk realized too late was that ultimately the only person we can change is ourselves. And when we change, the people around us will change in response to our new behavior.

5. Whatever *includes anything you are called to do by God.* I'm referring to specific assignments God has for you under the larger umbrella of the Great Commandment and Great Commission. For example, you are generally commanded to love everyone everywhere. But in a practical and personal way God may call you to focus some of your love on a grouchy clerk where you shop regularly or on an elderly neighbor who has no family or friends. Underneath God's encompassing command to share Christ with the world He may direct you specifically to witness through teaching a third-grade Sunday school class, giving generously to support a citywide evangelistic crusade, or participating in a short-term mission trip.

6. Whatever *includes fulfilling your purpose in life.* Why are you here on earth? What were you put here to accomplish? If you're a Christian, you likely embrace a general purpose something like the one summarized in the Westminster Shorter Catechism: "The chief end of man is to glorify God and enjoy Him forever." But what does that really mean?

In his excellent book *The Purpose-Driven Life,* Rick Warren, pastor of Saddleback Church in Southern California, contends that God has a fivefold purpose for every person He created. A large segment of the "whatever" in our life encompasses these five purposes.

First, we were "created for God's pleasure." We fulfill this aspect of our God-given purpose through *worship,* not only in the sanctuary but in the many and diverse activities of our everyday life as we glorify God by living obediently to Him.

Second, we were "formed for God's family." God has purposed that we are to be involved in intimate *fellowship* with a local group of believers—such as a church or a Bible study group—for mutual caring, learning, and support.

Third, we were "created to become like Christ." God desires that every Christian be involved in the process of *discipleship,* growing stronger and more mature through all life's seasons and circumstances.

Fourth, we were "shaped for serving God." Every Christian has been gifted and commissioned by God for specific *ministry* in the body of Christ, using our spiritual gifts to build up and assist other Christians in some way.

Fifth, we were "made for a mission." It is God's design that every believer be involved in *evangelism*, sharing the good news about Christ with others.[4]

Everyone is different, so your approach to fulfilling your God-given purpose will look a little different from everyone else's approach. Your purpose in life relates to your core values, unique abilities, specific calling, and deepest passions. Eric Liddell said he was created to run and to serve God in China. Lance Armstrong would probably insist that he was born for bicycle racing. Frederick Buechner said, "Purpose is the place where your deep gladness meets the world's need."[5]

Without a purpose fueled by passion, nothing in life matters. You can work sixty hours a week, maintain your home and family, and develop dozens of good hobbies and habits. But if you don't have a purpose for your efforts, you will lack the emotional and spiritual energy to continue, and your success will mean little to you.

I can think of nothing worthwhile in life that was achieved without great passion. Why bother doing anything if you are not headed toward something you feel God has called you to do? Once you have a vision for your life, passion is the spark that ignites you to reach your goal. That kind of purpose and passion will last a lifetime.

In a nutshell, how would you describe your purpose? Your answer to that question has much to do with what your life is all about. Whatever your purpose is, God calls you to do it passionately. Passion is the inner spark, provided by God's Spirit, that ignites you to live out your God-given purpose. A purpose not fueled by inner drive and enthusiasm is mere drudgery. The more you understand about why you take up space on this planet, the more you need the inner fire of passion to live out that purpose.

I'm happy to tell you I feel blessed to get up every morning and feel intense excitement about the work God has given me. It also brings me joy to see that my children are either doing what they love or are preparing to do what they love. When we're doing what we were meant to do, we can be certain God smiles.

But for some reason, many people believe that their passions run counter to the purposes of God. They can't imagine that He would want them to have fun or experience fulfillment. It never occurs to them how their desires got inside them in the first place. Yet the psalmist said, "Delight yourself also in the LORD, and He shall give you the desires of your heart" (Psalm 37:4). You can be certain that God would never give you those desires unless they were in accordance with His own. He designed you for a purpose, and He instilled the desires to match.

My youngest son, Daniel, could describe this principle from his own experience. Daniel went to college on a football scholarship. When he finished his education he was hired by ESPN, the sports network. He knew he had a job most young men would die for. Every weekend he flew from San Diego, where he lived, to the venue of the Sunday Night Football game. He was working beside Joe Thiesmann and Paul McGuire in the broadcasting booth as he learned the ropes of sports broadcasting production. He was elated until he discovered that he lacked a passion for sports production. He was drawn to the game, not to the broadcast. His true dream was to get involved with an NFL team and learn the ins and outs of management.

One day Daniel and I were talking it over. I urged him to follow his dream, no matter what that might be. Daniel began to pursue his passion, and now he is on the staff of the Baltimore Ravens NFL team. He was serious enough about his dream to put his house on the market with a sixty-day escrow. This made his dad a little nervous; I thought he might be jumping the gun. I wondered if I had advised him correctly.

But Daniel was in tune with his passion and God's plan. His house closed on the very weekend he began his new job with the

Ravens. That weekend also happened to be the deadline for letting ESPN know his status with them. Daniel's faith exceeded mine because only he knew the dream that God had instilled in him.

SPLIT DOWN THE MIDDLE

I find it sad—and disturbing—that many people today have segmented their passion. For example, some self-designated super-spiritual saints are only passionate about activities related to their spiritual life. They're in church every time the doors open. They are diligent about prayer and Bible study. They have read all the latest Christian bestsellers. And you'll hear nothing but Christian entertainment coming from their televisions, radios, and CD players.

All of those things are very good. I wish that every human being would pursue the spiritual life diligently. But as the old saying goes, it's possible to be so heavenly minded that we are no earthly good. This lopsided passion for the things of God doesn't extend to the "secular" side of their life—and to the lost souls God is passionate about.

Some people are passionate about church attendance, but somehow they have little interest in building relationships with neighbors who need their help. Some are zealous about preaching to others while lacking integrity at work. Some study the Bible thoroughly but ignore developing themselves through continuing education or donating time to civic activities. There is everything right about being passionate for the spiritual life, but there is something wrong if that's the only arena where passion is applied.

At the other end of the spectrum we find people who are passionate about everything *except* the things of God. These individuals are model citizens, their neighbors love them, and they are star performers at work. They are active in the PTA and the United Way. They are attentive parents who coach their kids' soccer teams. They consistently win salesperson-of-the-month awards because they are goal setters who just won't rest until they close the deal.

But when it comes to spiritual things, these people are just not very passionate. When you ask them why, they may give you a revealing answer: "Frankly, most churches I've been part of are pretty boring. I find much more excitement and passion outside the church."

Ouch! As much as I hate to admit it, I understand what they are saying. There are a lot of passionless people in our churches because there are a lot of passionless churches out there.

Why the dichotomy? Why do we find some people who are passionate only about their church life and others who are passionate about everything in life except the spiritual dimension?

At least part of the reason is an unbiblical division of the sacred from the secular—as if God created two separate worlds. We think of the sacred as God's part and the secular as our part. Then, depending on our motivations, values, and choices, we become passionate about one or the other. All too rarely do we meet Christians who are equally passionate about *all* of life.

I have news for you: All truth is God's truth, and all life is God's life. He didn't specially create "church people" to live separately from "others." He created one human race, of which He loves every last member. He doesn't set His eyes only on the church. His eyes roam to and fro across the nations, gazing at every one of us. His concerns are wide open, and your life should be no more or less than a reflection of that fact. His love, forgiveness, and grace are wide open. He longs to have fellowship with every last one of His children. If you follow your passion, it will lead you away from your church building and into the world. It might lead you to a television network or an NFL team, as it did my son. It might lead you to the Olympics and on to China, as it did Eric Liddell. It might lead you no farther than the end of your block.

But be certain of this: God has given you all the ingredients for a joy beyond description, beyond your imagining. Those ingredients are simmering inside you, bubbling to the surface. Can't you feel it? It's called your passion. Pursue God and pursue your passion wherever they may lead you, and you're certain to find unspeakable joy.

3

LIFE
UNLEASHING *the* POWER

WIDE
of a PASSIONATE LIFE

OPEN

You Gotta Have Heart

L IKE MANY KIDS HIS AGE, Will wandered through the jungle of
adolescence with no clue about what to do with his life. He was
sharp and intelligent, though more than a few at his school snick-
ered because he was quiet and scholarly. Will didn't pay much
attention to them; he was deep into his books of science, history,
world travel, and adventure. His room resembled a lab experiment
gone awry, cluttered with specimens of plant and insect life.

But even quiet, studious teenagers need a little pocket change.
Will found an entry-level job in a shoe shop. That was his life—
reading, puttering with his specimens, and selling shoes. But in time
he realized that it wasn't enough. He knew that if he had all the
books in the world, all the scientific knowledge attainable, and all
the money he could earn, there would still be a hunger inside him.
There were questions his science books couldn't answer. A shelf of
history offered no clues about the meaning of life. Will had
followed his passions but found they couldn't satisfy him.

At eighteen, Will left his parents' church in search of a livelier
and more fulfilling Christian fellowship. He found what he was
looking for in a little congregation in a neighboring town. His faith
in God sparked to life and began to grow, slowly but surely. Being
an ardent reader, Will devoured the Bible while continuing to read

volumes of books about the world around him. He began to think about the ideas in the Bible.

In the meantime, his shoe business was flourishing, and Will opened a store of his own. Yet he continued to sense that life must hold more for him—he was certain of that.

In his early twenties, Will married a lovely woman. He tried the life of a preacher then the life of a teacher. But he lacked those skills and still couldn't decide how to focus his life. He finally turned back to the shoe shop—which, of course, looked more like a bookstore with Will's library filling the shelves. The volumes kept coming, and so did the forming of Will's mind. He taught himself Greek, Hebrew, Latin, Italian, Dutch, and French.

Then, during his late twenties, the vision for Will's life came into focus. He was fascinated by a book about the last voyage of the great navigator and explorer Captain James Cook. To many people it was a thrilling story of adventure. But to Will it was a revelation of human need. While sketching a crude map of the world, he realized that there were vast numbers of the earth's population who had never heard about Jesus Christ. It occurred to him that if all people must believe in Christ to be saved, then that placed a crucial burden on every believer. Those who hadn't heard about Jesus would never hear unless some believer told them.

It was a simple but profound truth. If a man knew Christ and was serious about knowing Him, then the very meaning of his life was clear: He must tell as many others as possible. Suddenly the books, the shoes, the scientific pursuits—all of these things were swept aside in favor of a new, controlling passion. Will followed his passion resolutely until his death at age seventy-three, and we remember him today as the father of modern missions.

"Will" is better known as William Carey, shoemaker by trade, scholar and missionary by God's training. In the late eighteenth century in England, Carey was overwhelmed by the need for worldwide evangelism, and he committed himself wholeheartedly to that work. In 1793, at age thirty-two, William Carey set off with his family for India, where he devoted his entire life to sharing the gospel. Utilizing his skills and resources as a linguist, Carey played a major role in translating the Bible into more than forty languages.

William Carey is a sterling example of the passion principle in Colossians 3:23–24. We are called to do what we do "heartily"— wide open, pedal to the metal, no holds barred, no turning back. Burdened as a young man by the plight of the lost, Carey sobbed to God, "Here am I; send me." Then, after pouring out his life in whole-hearted service to Christ, he uttered from his deathbed, "When I am gone, say nothing about Dr. Carey. Speak about Dr. Carey's God." During the forty years between those two statements, William Carey lived out his purpose with sustained, heartfelt passion.

"But wait just a minute," you may argue. "If committing to passionate living means I have to spend the rest of my life toting Bibles through some bug-infested jungle, I'm not sure I want to sign on." If that's what you're wondering, you can relax. William Carey spent his life taking the Word of God to India because that's what God gifted and called him to do. Being a missionary to India was Carey's primary "whatever." The passionate life God has for you will center on your "whatever"—the combination of your gifts and talents and God's unique call on your life. And as you move into your life with passion, you will find as much satisfaction and fulfillment as William Carey did in India.

CAN YOU HEAR THE HEARTBEAT?

The passion principle in Colossians 3:23–24 admonishes us to do whatever we do "heartily," as if doing it for God Himself. What does *heartily* mean? In the New International Version of the Bible, the verse reads, "Work at it with all your heart." The strength of the passionate life is pouring our heart and soul—our very life— into what we do. Author Richard Leider commented, "Our world is incomplete until each one of us discovers what moves us—our passion. No other person can hear our calling. We must listen and act on it for ourselves."

Compare this image with the ways we sometimes describe how people approach their responsibilities. We say things like, "He gave only a halfhearted effort" or, "Her heart wasn't in it." The actions of these people communicate, "I'll give it all I've got . . . if I feel like it" or, "I'll work like a trooper . . . whenever the boss is watching" or, "I'll live out my commitment . . . unless something better comes along."

Had Lance Armstrong or Eric Liddell approached athletics with this attitude, there would have been no Olympic medals or Tour de France trophies for them. And had William Carey taken a half-hearted view of his mission, forty language groups in India would have had to wait a generation or more to read the Scriptures in their own language.

We also need to distinguish between momentary passion and everyday passion. We all experience spikes of emotional fervor, flashes of inspiration, and mountaintop highs when we are deeply passionate about a task or a project. For example, you see a great idea on television for redecorating the family room, so you rush out to buy supplies then stay up all night painting the walls. But six months later you still haven't finished the baseboards or remounted the switch plates. Your passion for redecorating came and went in less than twenty-four hours.

Or you come home from a church retreat gung-ho to get up a half-hour early every morning to read your Bible. For the first two weeks you don't miss a day. Then one morning you hit the snooze button once too often. The next weekend you skip reading the Bible altogether. A month after the retreat you are back to your old way of catching a few verses when you can fit them in.

If you try to maintain bursts of emotional and spiritual fire-works over the long haul, you will probably burn out a circuit. It's not healthy to live at a fever pitch all the time. Life wide open is a relatively steady, sustained effort of everyday passion. It's okay to burn the midnight oil on a decorating or fix-up project occasionally, but most tasks are better served by consistency, by plotting the course and sticking with it to its conclusion. The Liddells and Armstrongs of the world may sprint for position at times during a race, but a strong, sustainable pace is usually what wins. Everyday passion maintains momentum and persists at the task even when the emotions of momentary passion are absent.

What is that "sustainable passion"? I believe the clue is found in Colossians 3:23. You'll remember that verse reads, "Whatever you do, do it heartily, as to the Lord and not to men." The word *heartily* is often translated as soul or life. It means "from the very soul"—that is, life wide open. Let's follow that word as it turns up in other New Testament passages and we'll begin to understand what Paul has in mind.

For example, in Matthew 22:37, Jesus tells us all the commandments are embodied in two: to love the Lord with all our heart, soul, and mind; and to love our neighbors as ourselves. Jesus is underlining the point that we must love God and others from the deepest part of ourselves. Heart, soul, and mind mean we love people with everything we have. We love them passionately.

Then, in Mark 8:35–36, Jesus tells us that "whoever desires to save his life will lose it, but whoever loses his life for My sake and the gospel's will save it. For what will it profit a man if he gains the whole world, and loses his own *soul?*" (emphasis added). Again, the soul is the deepest and most profound essence of who we are. It runs so deep that you could gain all the possessions of this world and your soul would be lost—for all your attention would be outward on those possessions, rather than on the depths of the soul.

Third, in Matthew 11:28–29, Jesus says, "Come to Me, all you who labor and are heavy laden, and I will give you rest. Take My yoke upon you and learn from Me, for I am gentle and lowly in heart, and you will find rest for your *souls*" (emphasis added). Have you had a deep, soul-refreshing rest lately? Only Jesus can set at ease the very deepest part of you with the peace that surpasses all understanding.

Jesus lives in those depths, and He is Lord of them. Whatever we do, as Paul tells us in Colossians, we should perform the task with *soul*—from the very essence of who we are; with our heart, soul, mind, and strength; and with Jesus as the Lord of that action.

That's soulful living—life wide open.

A HEART OF SACRIFICE

Yes, Jesus brings peace and rest. But never forget that living life wide open—*soulfully*—will cost something. Ask anyone who has pursued his passion. Ask the Olympic athlete. Ask the dedicated artist who starved for her craft. Ask the young man who worked his way through college by waiting tables at night then studying until dawn because he had a passion for a college education.

A life of passion is a life of sacrifice. When you invest yourself wholeheartedly in your relationships, your work, and your service for Christ, your head will hit the pillow every night with that pleasing, soulful kind of fatigue. You will rest in the satisfaction that you have given a good effort, in the power and resources God supplies, at whatever you tackled during the day. But you have sacrificed. You have poured out your heart, soul, mind, and strength; and your resources are low.

The apostle Paul calls us to be a living sacrifice, "holy, acceptable to God" (Romans 12:1). He's talking about much more than giving up television or chocolate milkshakes for Lent, though such acts are meaningful for some people. Presenting ourselves as a holy sacrifice means placing ourselves on the altar before God—again, from the very *soul*. We reserve nothing. We attach no strings. And yet every ounce of our humanity tells us to be selfish, to be the captain of our own soul. It hurts to climb up on that altar, doesn't it?

William Carey found his passion, but he also found his price. Carey sacrificed a comfortable life in his native England to spend forty-one years in India. Once he was passionately involved in his mission, Carey had little time or interest for anything else. A typical day for him included reading from the Hebrew Bible and Greek New Testament, prayer, studying foreign languages, translating the Scriptures, correcting proof sheets of translations, teaching languages in a local college, and preaching. His Great Commission impact was staggering, with spiritual repercussions that echo through history to this very day—but he gave up many pleasures and lesser passions to make that true.

Do you think Paul made such sacrifices? That word *heartily,* used as *soul* or *life,* turns up again, and it demonstrates the price that must be paid. Paul said, "Chains and tribulations await me. But none of these things move me; nor do I count my *life* dear to myself, so that I may finish my race with joy" (Acts 20:23–24; emphasis added). That *life,* or *soul,* is what we give from the depths of ourselves, and giving it is not easy. But the joy is there nonetheless.

Here is the word yet again, in 1 John 3:16: "By this we know love, because He laid down His *life* for us. And we also ought to lay down our *lives* for the brethren" (emphasis added). Jesus gave all He had to give. He prayed to God from the depths of His soul at Gethsemane, and then He gave to us from the depths of His soul at Calvary. It was painful beyond our imagining—pain that shook the earth, darkened the skies, and caused the heavens to weep. But it was the sacrifice required by His passion to save us from an eternity of darkness. Jesus poured out His soul on the cross for us. He gave Himself unreservedly—heart, soul, and mind.

And what about Christians who gave their life for their faith? John uses our soulful word yet again as he describes a voice from heaven: "And they overcame him by the blood of the Lamb and by the word of their testimony, and they did not love their *lives* to the death" (Revelation 12:11; emphasis added).

Life. Soul. Sacrifice. I hope you can see by now that as fine a word as *heartily* is, it doesn't begin to capture the profundity of the power Paul is describing when he speaks of how we are to live. It would come much closer to say, "Whatever you do, do it passionately, soulfully, and give it all you've got to give, from the inside out." Or we could put it in the words of Mike Nappa, who described the life wide open:

> I've got news for you. True Christianity, courageous Christianity—the kind the apostles Paul and Peter and thousands of other early Christians practiced—isn't for wimps. It's not for the fainthearted, the lukewarm, the moderately committed, or the occasional church-goer. It's for the passionate, the ones with the courage to say, "I believe God, and I will dedicate my every waking hour to His purpose, no matter what it costs."[1]

That's soulful sacrifice. And it's worth every drop of blood, sweat, or tears.

LIONHEARTED PASSION

Do you remember Eric Liddell's fierce rival in *Chariots of Fire?* His name was Harold Abrahams, played by British actor Ben Cross. Abrahams was portrayed in the film not as a passionate runner but as a driven runner. He ran with a chip on his shoulder, a Jew with something to prove to the world. Abrahams was gifted with speed, but he strove to run with discipline and precise form. He was also a gold medalist at the 1924 Olympic Games.

There was a big difference in style between the precision of Harold Abrahams and the passion of Eric Liddell. Eyewitnesses to Liddell's running revealed that he ran with wild abandon. To put it kindly, Liddell didn't win Olympic medals because of his picture-perfect form. He ran straight up, head tilted back, knees churning high, arms flailing, mouth agape—as if his body could barely keep up with the joyful passion racing within. Eric Liddell didn't compete for style points; he ran to win and to relish the pleasure of the One who had made Him *fast*.

Passionate people live wide open, holding nothing back, because their purpose in life is defined in terms of passionately doing what they love. As comedian Bill Cosby said, "When you're younger, you want to be sure that by the time you're eighty years old you can sit on the bench and look back and say, 'Man, I did it all. I didn't miss a thing.'"

Passionate people would rather fail at something they love than succeed at something they hate. They define success in terms of excitement, enthusiasm, adventure, and joy. It never crosses their mind that what they do for a living is something others would call "work." It's something that comes up from the very depths of who they are. Passion has infused what they do with joy. As British preacher Charles Spurgeon said, "It is not how much we have, but how much we enjoy, that makes happiness."

I believe joy is a significant ingredient of a life wide open. There is risk, there is sacrifice, and there is pain; but there is always joy— the greatest signpost for God there could ever be. When you struggle to keep your home together yet praise God with joy, the world can see Him in you. When you lose your job and say, "The Lord is good; He will provide," then your faith is validated. And when you can show the world a life wide open, no holds barred, played out from the very depths of your heart, soul, and mind, the world sees your joy and understands who lies behind it.

Happiness? That's a lesser passion. It comes and goes, fickle as it is. But joy—now there's something worth pursuing. Heartfelt, life-giving, soulful joy knocks on the door of our heart one day and comes to live within us forever. To turn Jesus's statement upside down, you can lose the world and all its possessions, and your soul is intact. Your joy is still burning like an eternal candle. And you see that there are no other passions that can measure up to the passion for God.

Helen Keller never saw a candle. Blind and deaf, she lived in darkness. But she understood the light that no eye can see. She once said, "External conditions are the accidents of life, its outer trappings. The great enduring realities are love of service. Joy is the holy fire that keeps our purpose warm and our intelligence aglow. Resolve to keep happy and your joy and you shall form an invincible host against difficulty." Imagine that: you and your joy, standing together against any trial or difficulty.

If you're a teacher, allow a soulful passion for teaching to deepen your students' thirst for knowledge.

If you're an electrician, sense God's pleasure as you apply your skill to wiring a house or installing light fixtures.

If you're a lawyer, be lionhearted about securing justice for your clients.

If you're a spouse and a parent, nurture your dearest ones with all your heart.

If you're a preacher, pour your heart and soul into every sermon, every hospital visit, every meeting, and every prayer.

I've studied the lives of men and women throughout history who have left great spiritual legacies. I have discovered that those who have had the most profound impact on their world for the cause of Christ were those who followed their calling passionately. They did what they did with everything they had of energy, enthusiasm, and hard work. They poured themselves out upon the world as an offering from God. And in most cases, they were not necessarily the best or the brightest, the fastest or the strongest.

I'm convinced that if you are not passionate about what you are doing, you will not reach your God-given potential. From God's point of view, the greatest waste in life is the gap between what you are and what you could be. On the other hand, you can succeed at almost anything for which you have unbridled enthusiasm.

In contrast to the famous Nike motto, don't ever "just do it." Whatever you do, do it full throttle, with enthusiasm, energy, sacrifice, joy, and love. Those who run the race of life with passion always finish as winners.

4

LIFE
UNLEASHING *the* POWER

WIDE
of a PASSIONATE LIFE

OPEN

Who's It All For?

JACK WELCH, FORMER CEO OF GENERAL ELECTRIC, is regarded by many as the best corporate manager of the twentieth century. What was his secret? I suspect it was his motivational ability. His personal passion to succeed was contagious. Here's what Welch said about his passion and desire in business: "For me, intensity covers a lot of sins. If there's one characteristic all winners share it's that they care more than anyone else. No detail is too small to sweat or too large to dream. Over the years, I've always looked for this characteristic in the leaders we selected. It doesn't mean loud or flamboyant. It's something that comes from deep inside. Great organizations can ignite passion."[1]

You might even say that Welch modeled "business wide open." His employees knew he gave his all to every detail, and he expected them to work to his standards. After a while, the entire organization was excelling at a higher level than ever before.

Passion for the business was so important to General Electric under Welch that it was the company's practice to release the bottom 10 percent of its employees each year. If your annual performance review placed you at the lowest level of those in your evaluation group at GE, chances were good that you wouldn't be around for next year's review. You may have been a good performer

31

for another company, but if you couldn't muster enough passion to make it into General Electric's top 90 percent, you were history.

In any task, we work with a passion that reflects how we feel about the one we work for. That is, if you deeply admire your boss, you go the extra mile. But if you think he's a snake in the grass or a heartless slave driver, you'll never give your best. We find this is true for football coaches, American presidents, military leaders, schoolteachers, or anyone else who leads us through the testing grounds of life. Good leaders motivate us because of who they are. People come out of the woodwork to be a part of what these leaders are doing. If they have passion, we have passion.

Working for the Big Boss

David Seamands, author and professor at Asbury Seminary, tells a story about his seminary's cafeteria, which shared facilities with a college campus. One day, as the students moved through the lunch line, they found a basket of bright red apples. A sign placed by the staff read, "Take only one please—God is watching." The students progressed through the line, selected their courses, and reached the other end, where they found a box of broken cookies. There was another sign, this one hastily scrawled on notebook paper, clearly left by a student. This one read, "Take as many as you want. God is watching the apples."[2]

We chuckle because we understand that God is watching indeed, but He has no blind spot. He is watching the apples, the cookies, and everything else. Most of all, God is watching *us*. How often do we consider that fact? How much of a difference would it make in the lives of you, your family, your friends, and your coworkers if you lived with that message in mind all the time: *God is watching*. Perhaps you would find that to be a crushing burden. But perhaps, if you knew who God really is and understood His love and His grace, you would instead live passionately and wide open. If God is watching—and smiling upon you—then you would want to please Him every moment. If God is watching—and loves that hurting person in the next cubicle—then you would want to minister to that person to please God even more.

The apostle Paul knew that God is watching. He challenged us in Colossians 3:23–24 to do everything passionately, "as to the Lord and not to men." We work as to the Lord at the office, but that's only the beginning. We work as to the Lord while grouting the bathroom tile. We work as to the Lord when we stand to sing in church and when we change a diaper in the church nursery. There is no task in this world you cannot perform with passion, as long as you remember who that task is for and all that He has already done for you. How you do it will reflect how you feel about your Master.

That's the very reason history is filled with heroes of only average ability—people who understood that achievement is not the sum of what you have and what you do, but what you *bring*—from inside you. Michael Jordan, as most people know, was cut from his high school basketball team. Yet he became the greatest player in the history of his sport because of his passion for the game.

Brother Lawrence is more seldom celebrated, for he lived with a group of Carmelite monks in seventeenth-century Paris. He was no deep thinker or learned theologian. But he had a very special gift: an understanding that God was with him *everywhere*. That transformed everything about Brother Lawrence, and his writings on the subject have transformed countless others.

This particular monk, you see, was assigned to the kitchen. He cooked and cleaned for his Carmelite brothers. Kitchen drudgery? Not to him. Scouring every pot and rinsing every dish were extensions of his worship and service to God, as important as any other task in the monastery. He would pray, "Lord of all pots and pans and things . . . make me a saint by getting meals and washing up the plates!"[3] He would tell others, "The time of business does not with me differ from the time of prayer; and in the noise and clatter of my kitchen, while several persons are at the same time calling for different things, I possess God in as great tranquility as if I were upon my knees at the blessed sacrament."[4] He called it practicing the presence of God, and we could all use a little practice of that kind.

In the parable of the sheep and the goats, Jesus illustrated how our passionate good deeds go much further than the people for whom we do them. God, pictured in the story as a great king, says to His righteous servants: "Come, you blessed of My Father, inherit the kingdom prepared for you from the foundation of the world: for I was hungry and you gave Me food; I was thirsty and you gave Me drink; I was a stranger and you took Me in; I was naked and you clothed Me; I was sick and you visited Me; I was in prison and you came to Me" (Matthew 25:34–36).

The servants are puzzled. Their master has never suffered in any of these ways. They ask him to remind them when he, a king, was ever hungry, thirsty, lonely, or naked. And he replies, "Whenever you did one of these things to someone overlooked or ignored, that was me—you did it to me" (Matthew 25:40 MSG).

It's interesting that Jesus uses down-and-outers to illustrate that passionate service to others is, in fact, ministry to Him. Perhaps it's because we find it difficult to serve people who are dirty, disreputable, or potentially dangerous to us; it's easier to be passionate about helping people who *we* consider deserving. But as Jesus explained in the Sermon on the Mount, it's not up to us to make those kinds of evaluations. As long as the one who crosses our path is one who was created and loved by God, then we can be certain we must serve and love him too. And however we would wish to be treated, we can be certain we must treat that person the same way.

That principle, of course, is known as the golden rule, and again we look to Eugene Peterson for his memorable translation of Jesus's words in Luke 6:31–38 (MSG):

> Here is a simple rule of thumb for behavior: Ask yourself what you want people to do for you; then grab the initiative and do it for them! If you only love the lovable, do you expect a pat on the back?

Run-of-the-mill sinners do that. If you only help those who help you, do you expect a medal? Garden-variety sinners do that. If you only give for what you hope to get out of it, do you think that's charity? The stingiest of pawnbrokers does that.

I tell you, love your enemies. Help and give without expecting a return. You'll never—I promise—regret it. Live out this God-created identity the way our Father lives toward us, generously and graciously, even when we're at our worst. Our Father is kind; you be kind.

Don't pick on people, jump on their failures, criticize their faults—unless, of course, you want the same treatment. Don't condemn those who are down; that hardness can boomerang. Be easy on people; you'll find life a lot easier. Give away your life; you'll find life given back, but not merely given back—given back with bonus and blessing. Giving, not getting, is the way. Generosity begets generosity.

It would be wonderful to live that way, but how is it done? The golden rule sounds simple but proves difficult to live by. What is the secret to handling people as Jesus says we must handle them? For Brother Lawrence, it was an all-day, every-hour, wide-open passion for God. He experienced more joy in the kitchen than anyone with a million-dollar allowance at the world's finest luxury resort—because Brother Lawrence was with God, and that showed him the pots and pans in a whole new light.

William Carey gave his life to bringing God's Word to strange lands and people he didn't know, because he did it for God. As for Eric Liddell—let us briefly return to his story.

Liddell was favored to win the 100-meter dash in the 1924 Olympics, and the hopes of the British Isles were riding on him. But when a qualifying heat for the event was scheduled for Sunday, Liddell respectfully withdrew from the race. Sunday was the Sabbath for him, and that day was to be kept holy: no work, no sports. His country was counting on him to run, and he desperately wanted to run. But in his view, faith, and compromise could not coexist.

Liddell suffered fierce criticism because of his stand. Some of his countrymen suggested he was being disloyal to king and country. But in the film *Chariots of Fire,* an official at the Olympics says, "You see, him being loyal to his God is simply an extension of who he is. I'm glad there's somebody that still lives that way."

That's it! Eric Liddell's passion for running was an extension of his passion for God, not the other way around. And God rewarded him. He was given the opportunity to run in the 400-meter event—not his usual race—instead of the 100. He won the gold medal and set a world record.

We are empowered to live a truly passionate life when serving God is the object behind everything we do. Our passion is diluted when we live only to gratify self or win the approval of others. Peter and the other apostles of the early church made it clear who was at the center of their activities: "We ought to obey God rather than men" (Acts 5:29). The passionate ministry of these dedicated leaders resulted in thousands of people turning to Christ.

Paul wrote, "Do I now persuade men, or God? Or do I seek to please men? For if I still pleased men, I would not be a bondservant of Christ" (Galatians 1:10). Remember, Paul had been a very successful Pharisee, a well-educated man, a Roman citizen with every privilege that status entailed. Yet he gave it all up to live wide open, to follow his passion for Jesus Christ. He was consumed with that passion, and it gave him joy in every circumstance—even while sitting in prison or waiting for slow legal appeals when he wanted to be traveling and preaching. "To live is Christ," Paul said, "and to die is gain" (Philippians 1:21). There is no reason that you and I cannot live with such an unsinkable view of reality.

IT'S BONUS TIME

Consider this scenario: Your dad owns a billion-dollar business. One day he invites you to his office and says, "I plan to turn over everything to you, and I need you to work under me and learn the business. When I retire, it's your company—all of it. But in the meantime, you must follow my orders to the last detail. I'll be watching you like a hawk, and if you foul up, if you become lazy, if you try to do things your own way—then I'll leave you nothing at all."

Talk about a pressured life! There must be a better way to inherit an empire.

As a matter of fact, there is. Imagine that the same father said, "My child, I just wanted you to know it's all yours, no matter what. No strings, no trial period—the fact is that you're my child, I love you, and it gives me joy to pass on everything I own to you, both now and in the future. What I want most of all is to work closely with you, and I think you'll find that's the only way this business will work—you and I shoulder to shoulder. It's going to be trying at times, and you'll be rolling up your sleeves. This is going to be your life's work. But I don't look for perfection; I look for passion. And when you become weary and discouraged, just remember all that I've left you and that you and I are in this together."

I think we could all be excited about that proposition. I don't know about you, but my next words would be, "Where do I sign up?" That proposition is everywhere between the covers of your Bible. But the arrangement is even better.

Yes, we will "receive the reward of the inheritance" (Colossians 3:24). But we need not sweat and strain in order to be found worthy. We can't lose, for God has already called us His heirs. "Therefore you are no longer a slave but a son, and if a son, then an heir of God through Christ" (Galatians 4:7). That means every kingdom privilege is yours; all God can give you, He wants you simply to reach out and accept. Can you be passionate about living under those conditions?

But Colossians 3:24 speaks of an "inheritance." What is our Father leaving us in this will? It's not a secret locked up in a safe somewhere. No, the Bible gives us the details about what we have inherited. Paul wrote that he wants us to know "the riches of the glory of His inheritance in the saints" (Ephesians 1:18). Here are several characteristics of what God has already bequeathed to us.

37

1. *It is an "eternal inheritance"* (Hebrews 9:15). If you're fortunate enough to receive a substantial material inheritance from a relative or friend, it will only benefit you for this lifetime. And if you're not careful about your spending, it may not even last that long. The moment you die, anything left over belongs to someone else. But your inheritance from the Lord is eternal. It will last forever.

2. *It is "an inheritance incorruptible and undefiled and that does not fade away, reserved in heaven for you"* (1 Peter 1:4). What would you give for a financial portfolio that is impervious to inflation, theft, and stock market declines? Sadly, you can't get that kind of protection for your money here on earth.

3. *It is an inheritance with benefits in this lifetime.* Paul wrote, "And my God shall supply all your need according to His riches in glory by Christ Jesus" (Philippians 4:19). It's as if God has given us a debit card for the bank of heaven so we can draw on His provision on an ongoing basis. If we need courage, we make the withdrawal. If we need comfort, we have the spiritual funds. If we need wisdom, we can bank on it every time.

4. *It is an inheritance with benefits beyond this lifetime.* If you think it pays to serve Jesus now, just wait until you get to heaven. The Bible mentions a number of marvelous benefits that await us in heaven. Here are just a handful of them:

- Someday Christ will return for us, and from then on "we shall always be with the Lord" (1 Thessalonians 4:17).

- We will hear Christ say, "Well done, good and faithful servant; you were faithful over a few things, I will make you ruler over many things. Enter into the joy of your lord"(Matthew 25:21).

- We will receive the "crown of righteousness" (2 Timothy 4:8).

- We will receive "the prize of the upward call of God in Christ Jesus" (Philippians 3:14).

- We will receive a "reward," mentioned in Mark 9:41 and Hebrews 10:35.

- "We shall be like [Christ], for we shall see Him as He is" (1 John 3:2).

- We will be free of suffering, death, sadness, and pain (Revelation 21:4).

- We will be assigned positions of service and responsibility (Matthew 25:21–23).

- We will share Christ's glory (see Romans 8:17; 2 Thessalonians 2:14).

I don't know where you stand. You may be one of those people who hasn't decided about giving yourself fully to Christ. If that's the case, I have some bad news for you. Apart from trusting Jesus Christ for salvation, there is absolutely nothing you can do to earn the rewards I have described in the paragraphs above. Those rewards are offered to everyone but actually given only to those who reach out to take them.

You can't buy these rewards. You can't achieve them by being good. You can't earn them through church attendance or putting lots of money in the collection plate. God reserves His inheritance for His children, those who give their life to Him by receiving Christ as Savior. Why not open your heart to Him right now—not just for the benefits but because you'll never experience the fully passionate life He created you for apart from serving Him.

The change He will bring to your life is immeasurable, unimaginable, and incredible. Light will permeate every inch of what you see, as it did for the Christian woman in London who cleaned houses many years ago. As she entered each home, she would turn to her assistant and say, "Let's clean this house as if Jesus were staying here tonight."

That is the difference Jesus will make in your life. You might go to work and say, "Let's do this paperwork as if Jesus were going to be reviewing it." You might go to a meeting and say, "Let's conduct our affairs as if Jesus Himself were our guest of honor." The drudgery just fades away, and you work with joy—with passion.

Then will come the times when you are in deep need, deep danger, deep pain. And you will be able to say, "Let's approach this crisis as if Jesus Himself were beside me, holding my hand, protecting me." For it's true, of course. He is there, and if you have a very definite, very genuine, very passionate grasp of that fact, you will come through any storm that this life has to offer. How you will then live!

Last year our city, San Diego, hosted the Super Bowl, one of the biggest events of any year. We celebrated that weekend by inviting some Christian athletes to give their testimonies in our morning services. Our special guest speaker that morning was Bill McCartney, former coach of the Colorado Buffaloes football team and founder and president of Promise Keepers. During his message, Coach McCartney told a compelling story. I want you to hear it just as we did, in Coach McCartney's own words:

> The Illinois football team was going to play on Saturday for the Big Ten championship and the right to go to the Rose Bowl in Pasadena. The excitement and anticipation in Champaign/Urbana, Illinois, was sky-high because this game was at home and Illinois had not been to the Rose Bowl in twenty years.
>
> On Friday, the day before the game, a kid by the name of John Wong came up to his coach and said, "Coach, you've just got to let me start in tomorrow's game."
>
> The request startled the coach and he stepped back and said, "John, you're a great kid. You're a senior. You've done everything I've ever asked you to do. You're a tremendous student. But let's be honest. You play behind the captain of the team in your linebacker position, and you haven't started a game since you've been here. How can I put you in a starting role in a game of this magnitude?"

Big tears started streaming down Wong's face. "Coach," he said, "I know that's true, but you've got to start me!"

Well, the coach was moved and didn't know what to say, so he bought a little time and said, "I'll tell you what. Let me sleep on it. I'll have an answer for you in the morning."

You know, college football teams stay in hotels the night before the game, even for home games, and just by coincidence, John Wong's room was on the same floor as the coach's. Bright and early on Saturday morning, John Wong was pounding on the coach's door. He wanted an answer.

The coach came to the door and said, "I'll tell you what I'm going to do, John. I've thought about it and I've decided to put you in on the opening kickoff. That way, technically, you'll be starting the game. The stakes are very high and I can't promise you any more than that."

As fate would have it, Illinois kicked off that day, and John Wong ran down the field faster than anybody had ever seen him run. And he made a resounding tackle at about the eighteen-yard line. The captain started on the field, but the coach pulled him back and said, "After a hit like that, let's give him one more play."

On the first play from scrimmage, the opponent ran a trick play. The quarterback pitched the ball to the tailback. The tailback looked like he was going to sweep to the far side, then he stopped, planted his feet, and threw a pass to the quarterback sneaking out the back side.

Somehow, John Wong, who was playing linebacker, diagnosed the play, stepped in front of the quarterback, and intercepted the pass, running untouched into the end zone for a touchdown. The kicker missed the extra point. The game was not five minutes old and Illinois was ahead six to nothing.

John Wong continued to play, and he was all over the field. They had to substitute the captain at the other linebacker position because John Wong was dominating the game from his position.

The six-to-nothing score held up throughout the entire game.

[Then] the game was in the last minute. The opponent had the ball and time for one last play. The quarterback sent his fastest receiver down the sidelines and threw the ball as far as he could, hoping for a last-second miracle. And so help me, Wong retreated from his linebacker position, flicked the ball, and it fell harmlessly to the ground.

Champaign/Urbana, Illinois, erupted. Illinois was going to the Rose Bowl! The coach was carried off the field. As he got into the locker room, he looked over and in the corner all by himself was John Wong, crying like a baby.

The coach walked over and said, "John, what's the matter? You almost single-handedly won the game! No one has ever seen you play like that. What was going on out there?"

It took the kid awhile, but he gained his composure and said, "Coach, you know my daddy is blind."

"Of course I do," said the coach. "Many times your fraternity brothers have wheeled him onto the practice field so he could listen to us practice."

"Well," said John Wong, "my dad died Thursday night, and I figured this is the first time he had a chance to see me play."[5]

John Wong was playing his game for an audience of one, and it made all the difference in the world.

Now I can't vouch for the fact that the inhabitants of heaven can watch football games that are going on down here. But that's not the point of the story. What would happen to us if we really believed that Almighty God was watching "our game"? That's something I can affirm. He is!

5

LIFE
<small>UNLEASHING *the* POWER</small>
WIDE
<small>*of a* PASSIONATE LIFE</small>
OPEN

Draw Deeply from the Well Within

WHILE WE'RE ON THE SUBJECT OF PASSION, have you ever heard of passionfruit? You probably already know there's a tropical flower called the passionflower. It produces an egg-shaped fruit that looks something like a small pomegranate. Wouldn't it stand to reason that passion is the natural juice we extract from passionfruit, much like squeezing a delicious breakfast drink from an orange?

Well, not really. Of course you can't get *real* passion from a fruit. But just imagine how easy things would be if you could. We'd simply drive to the farmers' market, buy a nice crate of passion-fruit, and concoct a delightful fruit juice that would fill us with the drive we needed for life. Monday mornings would be a lot easier to face, wouldn't they? You'd get up bleary-eyed, yawning, and worrying about another week at the office—until you took a swallow of your passionfruit juice. Then you'd be ready to take on the world.

Before church, you could have a nice slice of passionfruit and go have an incredible spiritual experience. And a fruit like that would do wonders for any marriage.

If only we could put this stuff in a bottle. Much as the Spanish explorer Ponce de León scoured the bushes of St. Augustine,

43

Florida, searching for the Fountain of Youth, we would all love to find that bubbling fountain of passion that restores the gusto that somehow slipped away from us. We would dive right in and drink deeply, emerging restored and rejuvenated.

Unfortunately, you can't find passion on any shelf. You can't take dosages from a pill. You can't acquire it at the ritziest health resort or even pull it out of a book like this one. True passion comes from only one place. As Jesus said of the kingdom of God (see Luke 17:21), it is *within you.* It's like a cool spring buried beneath the surface, invisible but there all along. Should the explorer with the divining rod push his shovel into the right place, that fountain might spray forth into the air. Then a town could be built around that spring. There would be water for sustenance, for industry, and for agriculture. There can be no life without water.

The passion within you, if you could tap it, would burst from you just as dramatically, and you could build a vigorous, exciting, wide-open new life around that stream. As John G. Shedd said, it's better to be a geyser than a mud puddle.

In his best-selling book *Good to Great,* Jim Collins described the passion that is waiting to be discovered in all of us:

It may seem odd to talk about something as soft and fuzzy as "passion" . . . but throughout the good-to-great companies, passion became a key part. . . . You can't manufacture passion or "motivate" people to feel passionate. You can only discover what ignites your passion and the passions of those around you.

The good-to-great companies did not say, "Okay, folks, let's get passionate about what we do." Sensibly, they went the other way entirely: We should only do those things that we can get passionate about. Kimberly-Clark executives made the shift to paper-based consumer products in large part because they could get more passionate about them. As one executive put it, the traditional paper products are okay, "but they just don't have the charisma of a diaper."[1]

Let's call it by another word: *enthusiasm.* Og Mandino, author of *The Greatest Salesman in the World,* said, "Every memorable act in the history of the world is a triumph of enthusiasm. Nothing great was ever achieved without it because it gives any challenge or any occupation, no matter how frightening or difficult, a new meaning. Without enthusiasm you are doomed to a life of mediocrity, but with it you can accomplish miracles."[2]

The word *enthusiasm* comes from two Greek words: *en,* meaning "in" or "within," and *theos,* meaning "God." Enthusiasm, therefore, is "God within." That's a great way to describe the source of our passion. Passionate living is not only directed to Christ through whatever we do and whomever we serve, but the passion to do what we do comes from the Lord Christ within, in the person of the indwelling Holy Spirit. Christ is our passion because we were first *His* passion. As Erwin McManus pointed out:

> While a common definition of passion is "a compelling emotion or desire," the most unusual definition of passion is the sufferings of Christ on the cross. The second definition was for many years the primary definition in Webster's Dictionary. It is not incidental that the death of Jesus has come to be known as the Passion. The cross of Jesus Christ points to everything that God is passionate about. God the Son so passionately loves humanity that He was willing to give even His own life in our behalf. You know what you are really passionate about when you are willing to lay your life down for it.[3]

That wellspring of all that is good and pure and vital is placed within each of us—every human creature—by our Father. We look around us and see more people who live a life of quiet despair than of bursting passion. But all the same, every one of us has that fountain, that reservoir of living water. And there is a network of aqueducts extending from it to the outside world. Your words, your actions, your talents, and your gifts are pipelines of passion—God's pipelines to flood the world with His goodness and grace.

LIFE WIDE OPEN

I don't know if you're passionate about plumbing, but let's take a look at those two hydro-images: reservoirs and aqueducts. Let's think about how they bring living water to our world *through you*.

Tap Into the Reservoir

Eric Liddell's passion for running flowed from the deep reservoir of his passion for God. Liddell's commitment to Christ and to God's call on his life is even more visible after his triumph at the 1924 Olympic Games. Liddell kept his promise to the Lord and to his sister. After completing the university, he directed his full attention to ministry in China. More than a thousand well-wishers thronged outside the commissioning service held before the young missionary departed Edinburgh for China.

Think about it: Eric Liddell was only twenty-two years old when he walked away from the fame and fortune he might have achieved had he continued his athletic career. He might have been a force in international competition for many years, including the Olympics in 1928 and 1932. His countryman and rival sprinter, Harold Abrahams, made athletics his lifetime passion, distinguishing himself as a sports journalist, broadcaster, and leader of Great Britain's amateur sports establishment. But Liddell set aside sports for a greater passion: to serve God on the mission field.

Returning to China, Liddell taught science in the Anglo-Chinese College at Tientsin. Then he became a rural evangelist, taking the gospel throughout the region on foot and by bicycle. A brain tumor ended Eric Liddell's life at age forty-three, but not before he had lived out his passion for Christ on two continents.

Where does this kind of passion come from? As Liddell said in the movie *Chariots of Fire,* it comes *from within.* You may not have Eric Liddell's legs or lungs, but you have that same Spirit—that same source of amazing power and joy. Christ came to live within you permanently if and when you chose to love and follow Him. He came in the person of the Holy Spirit.

I believe it's important to examine what the New Testament tells us about the Spirit of God within you. Read these verses and reflect carefully about the nature of your indwelling. I have italicized key words for you to consider in each verse:

- Jesus said: "And I will pray the Father, and He will give you another Helper, that He may abide with you forever—the Spirit of truth, whom the world cannot receive, because it neither sees Him nor knows Him; but you know Him, for *He dwells with you and will be in you*" (John 14:16–17).

- Peter preached: "Repent, and let every one of you be baptized in the name of Jesus Christ for the remission of sins; and you shall *receive the gift of the Holy Spirit*" (Acts 2:38).

- Paul wrote: "Now hope does not disappoint, because the love of God has been *poured out in our hearts* by the Holy Spirit who was given to us" (Romans 5:5).

- Paul wrote: "But you are not in the flesh but *in the Spirit,* if indeed the Spirit of God dwells *in you. Now if anyone does not have the Spirit of Christ, he is not His*" (Romans 8:9).

- Paul wrote: "Now we have *received,* not the spirit of the world, *but the Spirit who is from God,* that we might know the things that have been freely given to us by God" (1 Corinthians 2:12).

- Paul wrote: "Or do you not know that *your body is the temple of the Holy Spirit who is in you,* whom you *have from God,* and *you are not your own?*" (1 Corinthians 6:19).

- Paul wrote: "And because you are sons, God has sent forth *the Spirit of His Son into your hearts,* crying out, 'Abba, Father!'" (Galatians 4:6).

- Paul wrote: "That good thing which was committed to you, *keep by the Holy Spirit who dwells in us*" (2 Timothy 1:14).

- Paul wrote: "Therefore he who rejects this does not reject man, but God, who *has also given us His Holy Spirit*" (1 Thessalonians 4:8).

The Spirit is always in us, but we are not always in the Spirit. The living water never runs dry, but we spend most of our life parched with thirst. The good news is that all you need, all you crave, all that would bring you the deepest joy, is already there. You need not spend a lifetime searching for it. If Christ is your Savior, the Spirit is your guest. And He longs to give you unspeakable joy and unquenchable passion.

The reservoir, then, is there, and it never runs dry—which is *not* to say we have no responsibilities toward that reservoir. He expects us to maintain the wellspring, to keep the waters flowing outward and to the world. The Spirit is within us, but we are to "be filled with the Spirit" (Ephesians 5:18). That is, we must see that the aqueducts to our inner reservoir are in operation.

Have you ever turned on a faucet in your home and discovered that somebody, perhaps working in your neighborhood, has turned off the pipes? It's an uncomfortable experience because we take water for granted. Every building, every facility used by people has to have access to water. God created us to drink water several times a day, as well as to use it for other purposes. Our body itself is made of a large percentage of water.

In the same way, we cannot afford to let the aqueducts of spiritual passion within us run dry. We need to open them—wide open! But how can we do that?

It is all there for the asking. Simply ask God to flood your heart with the Holy Spirit, to fill you to overflowing. That's one prayer He is eager to grant. It is inconceivable why so many of us seldom, if ever, make that simple request. He longs to flow in you and through you until the overflow drenches the world with His goodness and redemption.

I often pray something like this: "Dear Lord, I invite You to fill me with Your Spirit today so that I may live in the fullness of the power and passion You provide." I urge you to pray something similar on a daily basis. And whenever you find yourself in a situation in which you feel inadequate, call on the Holy Spirit to fill you again.

But there is also the issue of water pollution. How can the purity of the Holy Spirit ever be polluted? He cannot, of course, but those aqueducts can. Remember, they are made up of our words and actions and abilities—things that can quickly become contaminated by an unclean world. When we pollute the pipelines, we are grieving or quenching the Holy Spirit, as we read in Ephesians 4:30 and 1 Thessalonians 5:19. We grieve Him because He mourns over our disobedience and impurity. We quench Him because we dam up His natural flow to a dry, parched world.

Those aqueducts need to be wide open. We need to keep our inner reservoir of the Spirit full and fresh so that godly passion may burst through.

POURING OUT THE PASSION

What is the purpose of a pipeline? To transport water from one place to another. Think of your heart and soul as a hydroelectric plant whereby God moves between heaven and the world. Just as Christ was God in the flesh, now we are Christ in the flesh. We are His body. And what makes us so is the presence of His Spirit.

It's easy, then, to see how important those aqueducts are. God pours Himself into you so that you will generously pour yourself out to others. We are urged in Ephesians 5:18 to be filled continually with the Spirit because God intends us to be sharing His power and passion with those around us every day and in every way.

How does the life of passion flow from its source—the Spirit within you—to the world around you? Through the way God designed you—your God-given gifts and abilities. Each of us is completely unique in our natural abilities, just as no two sets of fingerprints match. Some of us are gregarious and outgoing while others are shy and quiet. Some people can sing like angels while others couldn't carry a tune if it had handles. There are those who can fix anything with a screwdriver and a roll of duct tape, and there are those who don't even know which end of a screwdriver to hold.

You already know what you do really well. Maybe you're a good listener. Perhaps you are good with numbers and details. Perhaps it's a talent such as singing or writing. Pour the passion of the Spirit into those natural abilities. Whatever it is that you do well, do it "heartily," soulfully, by allowing the indwelling Spirit to empower you.

Think of the living water, perfect and refreshing, flowing through millions of different faucets of every color, material, size, and design, all across the earth. That's the thought Paul expressed in 1 Corinthians 12:4–7: "There are diversities of gifts, but the same Spirit. There are differences of ministries, but the same Lord. And there are diversities of activities, but it is the same God who works all in all. But the manifestation of the Spirit is given to each one for the profit of all."

I imagine you've never pictured it this way, but we are a colorful collection of assorted pipes, aren't we? We all carry the same miraculous living water, but we deliver it to the world in our own unique way, based on how God designed us.

There are also very special aqueducts called spiritual gifts. Each of us has at least one, and it's our most powerful way to carry the grace of God to the world. Of course, it helps when we know our gift or gifts. According to the Barna Research Group, 69 percent of American Christians have heard of spiritual gifts but don't know what their own spiritual gifts are. How do you discover your unique gift or gifts?

Some churches offer spiritual gift analysis tests, and those can be helpful as you begin to discover the abilities and passions God has given you for ministry. You can also ask your friends and fellow worshipers for their opinions of your strengths and abilities. But perhaps the best way to unearth your spiritual gift is simply to *get busy*. Ask the Lord to show you how you should serve Him and then get involved in His work. It will become increasingly clear how He has gifted you as you grow in Christ, volunteer for various ministries at church, and find opportunities to extend and strengthen His kingdom.

Diamonds are unearthed from below, but spiritual gifts are dispensed from above. Just as diamonds are rough and uncut when first discovered, your spiritual gift may need to be developed and polished. But don't be discouraged; just get busy with the opportunity currently at hand, and you'll gradually grow more and more comfortable with what God has called you to do with the abilities He has given you.

Here's the way the apostle Peter put it: "As each one has received a gift, minister it to one another, as good stewards of the manifold grace of God. If anyone speaks, let him speak as the oracles of God. If anyone ministers, let him do it as with the ability which God supplies, that in all things God may be glorified through Jesus Christ, to whom belong the glory and the dominion forever and ever" (1 Peter 4:10–11).

A. T. Pierson, a Bible teacher from an earlier era, said: "Everyone has some gift, therefore all should be encouraged. No one has all the gifts, therefore all should be humble. All the gifts are for one Body, therefore all should be harmonious. All the gifts are needful, therefore all should be faithful."[4]

You may already have identified the spiritual gifts God has invested in you. If so, direct the passion of the Spirit within through those supernatural abilities in order to build up other Christians. If you don't understand how God has gifted you, begin a quest in the Word of God and prayer to discover the channels for the passion and power God has provided for you.

HOW CAN WE LIVE WITHOUT PASSION? How can we get through the dull days and the dark nights without the joy that is our birthright? We might as well be the children of a millionaire, living as paupers and rummaging in trash bins for our food—when a hearty feast is set out on the table of God all the time.

You need not wander through the streets to find that table. It is set and waiting within you. It is the bread of life. It is the living water that wells up from a heavenly spring that never runs dry. God wants you to find your passion so that others may find Him through it.

Open the aqueducts—wide open!

6

LIFE WIDE OPEN

UNLEASHING *the* POWER

of a PASSIONATE LIFE

A Fork in the Road

GENERAL LEW WALLACE was traveling by train when he came to his fork in the road. How can that happen when one is traveling on railroad tracks? It happens within. One moment can change more than your life; it can alter your eternity.

Wallace was casually chatting with a colonel named Ingersoll as the train steamed along. Neither of the two men counted himself as a Christian, but that day they were discussing the life of Jesus. Wallace said, "Myths and superstitions aside, I think His life would make a great novel."

Ingersoll immediately said, "I should say so, and you're just the man to write it. Once and for all, throw out all the hocus-pocus and show Him to be the plain, common man he undoubtedly was—a good man, but no more than that."

General Wallace took the advice. But somewhere along the journey of writing, his book took a fork in the road. So did the tone of his life. The more he read, the more he studied, and the more he reflected on the life of Jesus of Nazareth, the more convinced he became that Jesus was no plain, common man at all. *Truly this was the Son of God.* Wallace began in cynicism and finished in worship. His book, *Ben-Hur,* has become a classic.

Frank Morison was traveling in elite legal circles when he came to his fork in the road. He was a bright, articulate lawyer who started out with a passion to debunk the "resurrection myth" forever—and he completed his work with another passion entirely. He agreed with the fictional detective Sherlock Holmes that if the facts of a mystery are examined logically and every possible explanation is systematically eliminated, the one that remains must be the explanation, no matter how absurd or illogical it seems. Morison engaged in what his profession called "discovery of evidence" and came to the conclusion that Jesus Christ rose from the dead on the third day, beyond any doubt. The book he wrote, *Who Moved the Stone?*, is still considered a classic defense of the Resurrection.

But there is a third writer more extraordinary than either of these two—and at least this one, when he came to his fork, was actually on a road! His name was Saul, and passion coursed through his veins in a way the world has seldom seen. As a kind of ecclesiastical hit man for the Hebrew establishment, he sought out Christians and persecuted them with ruthless, uncompromising commitment. When he made the same discovery as Frank Morison and Lew Wallace—that the one he persecuted was, in fact, the Lord of life—he rose from the dust and traveled along a new road for the rest of his life.

It was Paul who gave us the passion principle in Colossians 3:23–24. For him, "whatever you do" was reaching the lost for Christ. Evangelism was at the core of his every thought, word, or deed. Paul serves as a pattern for passion in at least three areas. First, he shows what it means to be a sold-out, no-holds-barred servant of Christ. Second, he is a model of the character of a passionate servant of Christ. Third, he is a model of the ultimate goal of life—sharing Christ with others.

Let's soak up all we can from the remarkable story of the apostle Paul.

A Fork in the Road

SOLD OUT TO SERVE THE SAVIOR

Paul—or Saul, as he was called then—was galloping along with his fellow persecutors, salivating at the prospect of dragging more Christians off to jail. Then suddenly—*bam!*—he was on the ground, blinded by a powerful light. A heavenly voice asked, "Saul, Saul, why are you persecuting Me?" (Acts 9:4)

Saul answered the question with one of his own: "Who are you, Lord?" (v. 5). I've always thought it amazing that Saul answered his own question: *Who are you? Lord.* Those from the Jewish rabbinic tradition—which was Saul's background—understood any voice from heaven to be the voice of God Himself. I think Saul knew before he even hit the ground that his life was about to change dramatically.

Nothing reveals more about how Paul saw himself after his conversion than the way he frequently identified himself: "Paul, a bondservant of Jesus Christ" (Romans 1:1). Not "Paul, the pedigreed former bigwig in the anti-Christian Gestapo." Not "Paul, the guy with the spectacular conversion experience." Not "Paul, the famous apostle to the Gentiles." Not "Paul, the author of most of the New Testament epistles." Just "Paul, a bondservant of Jesus Christ"—period.

When Paul met Jesus, he didn't merely assent to the Christian faith. He voluntarily became Jesus's bondservant. He gave the Lord everything he was and everything he had—his life and breath; his past, present, and future; his hopes and dreams; his passion for living.

Paul's voluntary servitude to his Lord is even more significant in light of his culture's laws concerning slaves. In those times it was common for poor people to sell themselves to the wealthy as slaves. In exchange for their labor they received room and board, and, if the master was kind, other benefits. For these people, being enslaved and fed was more acceptable than being free and starving.

Before Paul was born, Roman law stated that no Roman citizen who had been born free could be enslaved. But some unscrupulous people were taking advantage of this law for their own profit. For example, a working-class Roman citizen (we'll call him Marcus) sells himself as a slave into the employ of a wealthy, unwitting Roman landowner. Sometime after the deal has been done and the money exchanged, Marcus's accomplice, Gaius, approaches the landowner with papers proving Marcus's Roman citizenship. "Too bad, mister," says Gaius, "but Marcus is a citizen and, by law, cannot be enslaved. If you don't release him immediately, I'll call the authorities." Marcus and Gaius take the money and run, and there's nothing the hapless landowner can do about it. The two men are free to con other wealthy Romans in some other area of the empire.

Due to the adverse effect of this scam on the Roman economy, a new law was enacted just before Paul came on the scene. The law stated that any citizen who sold himself into slavery could no longer claim free status—not ever. This new law closed the loophole. Voluntary slaves became permanent, lifetime slaves with no recourse for freedom. It was with this backdrop that Paul, a Roman citizen, gave himself to Jesus as a servant for life. Paul was so passionate about serving Christ that he signed himself over once and for all. He lived what the hymn writer so eloquently declared: "The world behind me, the cross before me; no turning back, no turning back."[1]

Being a Jew, the apostle Paul was also keenly aware of Mosaic legislation concerning voluntary slavery. The Law allowed a slave who truly loved his master to declare upon being set free, "I love my master, my wife, and my children; I will not go out free" (Exodus 21:5). The Jewish slave who remained in voluntary submission to his master bore an identifying mark: "His master shall pierce his ear with an awl; and he shall serve him forever" (v. 6). Similarly, Paul, having suffered extensively in the passionate service of his Master, wrote, "I bear in my body the marks of the Lord Jesus" (Galatians 6:17).

The life of passion for the Christian begins with total surrender to the lordship of Jesus Christ. It is through presenting yourself to the Master voluntarily, unreservedly, and permanently that you unleash the power of the passionate life.

It's the ultimate fork in your road. You are a slave; you are a human sacrifice laid voluntarily upon the altar. You die to the old life so that you may be reborn to the new, wide-open life of Christ and all His power. You die in order to live, you become a slave in order to be free, and you give away the world in order to gain your soul.

THE SERMON OF YOUR LIFE

On December 1, 1955, a plainspoken African-American woman named Rosa Parks boarded a bus in Montgomery, Alabama, to ride home—or so she thought. She, too, came to the fork in her road. In her book, *Quiet Strength,* she wrote: "When I sat down on the bus that day, I had no idea history was being made—I was only thinking of getting home. But I had made up my mind. . . . I felt the Lord would give me the strength to endure whatever I had to face. It was time for someone to stand up—or in my case, sit down. So I refused to move."[2]

Though ordered by the bus driver to give her seat to a white man, Rosa Parks remained in her place. One thing led to another in her town and across the nation, and the legal conflict led to a ruling by the United States Supreme Court that racial segregation is unconstitutional.

Rosa Parks didn't seek—and never claimed—credit for launching the civil rights movement. She only wanted to do what was right. She was passionate about generations of African-Americans who had been denied their God-given and constitutional status as equals among other Americans. So she did something about it. A passion for others suffering wrong triggered in Ms. Parks a passion to do her part to make it right. That's godly character making a positive difference in the lives of others.

I believe Paul would have approved of the stand (or the seat) Rosa Parks took and the suffering she was willing to endure for it.

Paul cared a great deal about integrity. He didn't want his words to be devalued or rejected because he failed to practice what he preached. He lived at a high standard of character so that his actions would enhance, not detract from, his message.

For example, as an apostle, Paul had the right to be financially supported by the churches he served. It was a common, accepted practice among first-century Christians just as it is today—the congregation pays the minister by some means. Paul built a strong case for this protocol in 1 Corinthians 9:1–11. But instead of taking his due, Paul worked on the side as a tentmaker to earn his own support, and many of those with him took other jobs as well. He didn't want to be a burden to those he served, and he didn't want anyone to wrongly construe that he was in the ministry for the money, bringing reproach on the gospel he preached. Paul was passionate about maintaining godly character so that nothing would "hinder the gospel of Christ" (1 Corinthians 9:12).

Paul did not leave the development of godly character to chance. "Servant of Christ" was not just a title to him. He was passionate about serving his Master body, soul, and spirit. He wrote, "Therefore I run thus: not with uncertainty. Thus I fight: not as one who beats the air. But I discipline my body and bring it into subjection, lest, when I have preached to others, I myself should become disqualified" (1 Corinthians 9:26–27).

Like an athlete in training, Paul knew he had to be in world-class condition and play by the rules or he would be the laughing-stock of his event. If he was not passionate about developing strong, godly character, those who heard him would have every right to discount him and his message. And Paul was not about to let that happen.

Living wide open for God includes pursuing godly character with passion. And since godly character is really the character of God forming in us, we must rely on the work of the indwelling Holy Spirit to help us become a person of righteousness and integrity who reflects Christ. As Paul explained in Galatians 5, character building is the process of saying no to the flesh while allowing the Holy Spirit to cultivate His character—pictured as fruit—in our life: "But the fruit of the Spirit is love, joy, peace, longsuffering, kindness, goodness, faithfulness, gentleness, self-control. Against such there is no law" (Galatians 5:22–23). That fruit grows from a life of passionate devotion to Christ. When the world sees that fruit, it suspends its disbelief to hear our story.

GIVING YOUR ALL FOR OTHERS

Did you see the 1992 film version of James Fenimore Cooper's classic tale, *The Last of the Mohicans?* The movie includes a poignant scene of courage and passionate self-sacrifice. A British major and the two adult daughters of a British colonel have been captured by the Huron Indians, who are in league with the French against the British. The tribe is preparing to burn the two women captives at the stake as a sacrificial offering to the Huron chief.

At the last minute, Hawkeye, a Mohican Indian who is trying to save the women, steps up and offers to die in their place. Unable to communicate with the Hurons, Hawkeye tells the major to translate his request: "My death is a great honor to the Huron. Take me!" But instead of relaying Hawkeye's message to the Hurons, the brave major, speaking in the Huron tongue, offers himself as a substitute for the women and the Mohican.

By the time Hawkeye understands what the major has done, it's too late. Hawkeye, who had offered himself as a sacrifice, suddenly realizes that the major has given *himself* to be a sacrifice. As Hawkeye hurries the two women away from the Huron camp, the major is tied to the stake and set ablaze. From a safe distance, the stunned Mohican puts the major out of his misery with a single rifle shot.

Jesus said, "Greater love has no one than this, than to lay down one's life for his friends" (John 15:13). Great passion requires the ultimate in *com*passion. That's what makes Paul's desire to reach the lost so profound: He was one of only three persons in the Bible who offered to exchange his life for the salvation of others. Paul declared, "I could wish that I myself were accursed from Christ for my brethren, my countrymen according to the flesh, who are Israelites" (Romans 9:3–4).

Moses shared Paul's self-sacrificing passion for others. He asked God to blot him out of His book if the Lord did not forgive the idolatrous Israelites in the Sinai desert (see Exodus 32:32). God responded by forgiving the people. And Jesus, of course, not only offered His life but "gave Himself a ransom for all" (1 Timothy 2:6).

What did Paul mean by wishing to be accursed that Israel may be saved? He knew it wasn't possible for him to be cursed in Israel's place. But his heartfelt plea demonstrated his deep passion for those outside of Christ. He was willing to give up everything to reach his wayward countrymen, so he lived his entire life passionately in the face of painful opposition to share the gospel. Eventually Paul *did* give up his life for his faith, but not before bending every effort to bring unbelievers to the Master to whom he owed everything.

Henry Thoreau, the rugged New England nonconformist of the nineteenth century, once went to jail instead of paying a poll tax in his state, for he knew the tax supported slavery. Thoreau's good friend Ralph Waldo Emerson heard Thoreau was in jail and went immediately to visit him. Peering through the iron bars into the cell, Emerson exclaimed, "Why, Henry, what are you doing in there?"

The unperturbed Thoreau shot back, "Nay, Ralph. The question is, What are you doing out there?"

Paul was in prison numerous times for preaching the gospel. I can imagine a friend coming to visit him and posing Emerson's question: "Paul, what are you doing in there? Why did you allow yourself to get arrested for preaching the gospel?" And I can hear the apostle's bold response: "The question is, Why aren't you in here too? Where is your passion for the lost?"

That question rings true to me: What else can be more important than sharing the Good News with others?

Now, admittedly, you and I have not been called to the Gentiles as Paul was. Referring to the Gentiles, Jesus commissioned Paul "to open their eyes, in order to turn them from darkness to light, and from the power of Satan to God, that they may receive forgiveness of sins and an inheritance among those who are sanctified by faith in [Christ]" (Acts 26:18).

But just as surely as Paul was sent to preach the gospel to the Gentiles, you, too, have an assignment from God. As a Christian, you have been sent by God to share the good news with the people in your circle of relationships: family members, friends, coworkers, and neighbors. Paul wrote that God "has reconciled us to Himself through Jesus Christ, and has given us the ministry of reconciliation" (2 Corinthians 5:18).

Think of it. God came into the darkness at a great price—the price of His only Son—to rescue us and bring us back into His arms. Now He gives us the same task. We are to stride into the darkness and rescue as we were first rescued. Personally, I cannot imagine anyone who fully understands what Christ has done yet doesn't have a powerful passion to pass on that gift to others.

Paul's passion was great enough to land him in prison. And as you read this, there are Christians suffering all across the world because they dare to share their faith. Living *wide open* can lead you to a cell *tightly closed*. Even so, those who fully understand the depth and power of God's love for them march onward without hesitation. They know His power and grace will go with them—and be manifest most abundantly—when they dare to step into the darkness.

Jim Elliot was a passionate missionary and follower of Jesus who was killed by Auca Indians in Ecuador in 1956. He prayed, "Father, make of me a crisis man. Bring those I contact to decision. Let me not be a milepost on a single road; make me a fork, that men must turn one way or another on facing Christ in me." He had come to the fork in his road, and he wanted to personally become a fork in the roads of others.

He also wrote: "God, I pray Thee, light these idle sticks of my life, that I may burn for Thee. Consume my life, my God, for it is Thine. I seek not a long life, but a full one, like You, Lord Jesus." This was a man who understood passion—who wanted to live full throttle, nothing reserved, wide open, no matter what it cost him. And in the end, he was martyred at the hands of the Auca Indians. In so doing, he became a fork in the road not only to the many Aucas who later came into the kingdom of God through his example but also to countless believers who have been inspired by his story. The sticks of his life, as he put it, burned more brightly than he could ever have imagined.

Michael Card tells about a man named Joseph who shared that vision:

One day Joseph, who was walking along one of these hot, dirty African roads, met someone who shared the gospel of Jesus Christ with him. Then and there he accepted Jesus as his Lord and Savior. The power of the Spirit began transforming his life; he was filled with such excitement and joy that the first thing he wanted to do was return to his own village and share that same Good News with the members of his local tribe.

Joseph began going from door to door, telling everyone he met about the Cross of Jesus and the salvation it offered, expecting to see their faces light up the way he had. To his amazement the villagers not only didn't care, they became violent. The men of the village seized him and held him to the ground while the women beat him with strands of barbed wire. He was dragged from the village and left to die alone in the bush.

Joseph somehow managed to crawl to a water hole, and there, after days of passing in and out of consciousness, found the strength to get up. He wondered about the hostile reception he had received from people he had known all his life. He decided he must have left something out or told the story of Jesus incorrectly. After rehearsing the message he had first heard, he decided to go back and share his faith once more.

Joseph limped into the circle of huts and began to proclaim Jesus. "He died for you, so that you might find forgiveness and come to know the living God," he pleaded. Again he was grabbed by the men of the village and held while the women beat him, reopening wounds that had just begun to heal. Once more they dragged him unconscious from the village and left him to die.

To have survived the first beating was truly remarkable. To live through the second was a miracle. Again, days later, Joseph awoke in the wilderness, bruised, scarred—and determined to go back.

He returned to the small village and this time, they attacked him before he had a chance to open his mouth. As they flogged him for the third and possibly the last time, he again spoke to them of Jesus Christ, the Lord. Before he passed out, the last thing he saw was that the women who were beating him began to weep.

This time he awoke in his own bed. The ones who had so severely beaten him were now trying to save his life and nurse him back to health. The entire village had come to Christ.[3]

Passion is not cheap. But it is real; it is priceless. It may cost your life, but it will save your soul. Generations of believers, now passed from the earth, handed down the gospel so that you could hear it. Now it's your turn. You stand at a fork in the road—which way will you turn?

7

**LIFE
WIDE
OPEN**

UNLEASHING *the* POWER

of a PASSIONATE LIFE

Fire in Your Bones

Enrique "kiki" camarena grew up in Mexico in a house with a dirt floor. Though his upbringing lacked many modern advantages, Kiki's heart was filled with big dreams. Somehow he knew he was destined to make a difference. When he was just a child, he begged his mother for a toy gun because he said he was going to be a policeman when he grew up. At nine, the little boy with the big plans moved with his family to the United States to pick fruit.

After working his way through college and earning a degree in criminal justice, Kiki enlisted in the United States Marine Corps. After a successful stint in the military, he became a police officer and felt he could make a difference in society. But being a patrol cop wasn't enough. Remembering how many of his friends had turned to drugs in high school and how he had been tempted to do the same, he applied for a position with the United States Drug Enforcement Administration.

The DEA sent Kiki Camarena to his native Mexico to work undercover, investigating a large drug cartel that was believed to include Mexican military, police, and government officials. On February 7, 1985, Agent Camarena, then thirty-seven, left his office to meet his wife for lunch. But he never arrived. Five thugs accosted him as he left his office. They brutally forced him into a car and drove off. That was the last that was ever seen of Kiki Camarena, at least until his body was pulled from a shallow grave. He had been tortured to death by the people he wanted to help to a new, drug-free life.

But Kiki Camarena's death was not in vain. When the tragic news reached his friends and neighbors in the U.S., they adopted as a simple badge a ribbon of red satin to wear on their lapels in honor of his life and work. An organization called the National Family Partnership evolved from the grassroots efforts to honor Camarena, and the first Red Ribbon Campaign was organized in 1986. The campaign's message about drug prevention has reached millions of American children and has been recognized in the United States Congress.

When Enrique Camarena first told his mother that he wanted to leave police work and join the DEA, she tried to talk him out of it, afraid for his safety. His reply to his mother will ring true for all who have ever been consumed by vision and passion: "I *can't not* do this. I'm only one person, but I want to make a difference." Today millions of young people are hearing a message about drugs that might save their lives because Enrique Camarena couldn't say no to his passion.

"I *can't not* do this"—that's the power of passion in the human soul. Stories of the power of passion abound in our world. They cut across racial and social lines and know no boundaries. Passion is the echo of God's voice in the hallways of our soul. There are choices in life, and then there are passions—*compulsions*. It might appear to the world that we are making a choice, but we've known from the beginning we had only one option.

Why would any of us feel that way about a particular cause unless God instilled those feelings in us? Perhaps the greatest proof we have that God is alive and well is the reality of so many people taking exorbitant risks, going to extreme lengths, paying ultimate prices to fulfill some calling that others might overlook. If we are, as some scientists insist, no more than higher-level members of the animal kingdom—and *not* creatures of God, a little lower than the angels—then why are we passionate? Why do we seek to do great things for eternal causes? I know of no animal that ever died for a philosophy.

If this fire is in our bones, then who lit the match?

A PASSIONATE PROPHET

Like many of the prophets of old, Jeremiah was a stubborn, single-minded individual. You would have deeply respected him all the while he was driving you crazy. Jeremiah had a message from God, and he was going to deliver it no matter who got in his way. But he was as tender as he was tough, and the fountain of passion within often overflowed in the form of tears.

Passionate people are heartfelt people, filled with both joy and sorrow. So it's not surprising to discover that Jeremiah has been called "the weeping prophet." His passion to press for repentance resulted in a lifetime of pain interposed with accomplishment. He wept for the blindness of Israel. He wept for the passing of a great nation, for the legacy of David and Solomon. He wept, too, out of sheer frustration at a life spent calling out to those who could not seem to hear.

God had written upon Jeremiah's heart with fire, and Jeremiah's intense desire included intense frustration and grief. When you and I get to heaven, we can dry his tears, comforting him with testimonies of the enormous truths he taught us—truths such as these.

1. *Jeremiah's passionate, prophetic preaching was rooted in God's call.* God spoke to him pointedly when he was a young man, saying, "Before I formed you in the womb I knew you; before you were born I sanctified you; I ordained you a prophet to the nations" (Jeremiah 1:5). God reaffirmed His call to Jeremiah on numerous occasions (see 3:12; 7:2, 27–28; 11:2, 6; 13:12–13; 17:19–20).

You should always remember that God cherished His special

plans for you long before you were ever born. From the foundation of creation, before there was time itself, He knew you just as He knew Jeremiah. He knew every tiny fact there would someday be to know about you. He saved this one special task for you and then created your heart and desires as a matching set.

2. *Jeremiah resisted, but God persisted.* The God-appointed preacher disqualified himself, saying, "I cannot speak, for I am a youth" (1:6). But God qualified Jeremiah with a touch of His hand. Jeremiah wrote, "Then the LORD . . . touched my mouth, and the LORD said to me, 'Behold, I have put My words in your mouth' " (v. 9).

"What will I say?" you ask, paralyzed by fear. "I'm too young! I'm too inexperienced!" But God will never give you a job without the skills. He will never give you a goal without the means to get there. He is the equipper; all talents, means, and possibilities are in His hands. And He has promised to be with us always.

3. *God warned Jeremiah that there would be obstacles.* God told the prophet that those to whom he was sent "will fight against you" (v. 19). That's an understatement! Jeremiah was severely beaten, locked up in stocks, and publicly humiliated by the religious leaders of his day. The king cut up the scrolls containing Jeremiah's prophetic message and tossed the pieces into the fire. Jeremiah met resistance—sometimes very painful resistance—every step of the way. And like many before and after him, Jeremiah cried out in misery to God, "Why must it be this way? Why can't they see the truth?" The Lord softly tells us that pain comes with the territory. He reveals His nail-scarred hands to show us He understands how it feels.

If the tasks we set out to do were easy or assured, we wouldn't be passionate about them. They would be mundane tasks, and perhaps God could have them accomplished by committee. He certainly didn't envision you from the dawn of time and think, *This is a person for whom My greatest desire is that she be comfortable all her life and watch lots of television.*

We're not talking about mundane desires. We're discussing

dominions and authorities. We're talking about strongholds of sin and corruption. This is war, and that's why God has raised us up. That's why He equipped us with this passion in the first place. You can't march off to war with a yawn and a shrug.

You can be certain that if you try to accomplish anything righteous in this world, opposition will rise up to block your path. As Paul wrote, "All who desire to live godly in Christ Jesus will suffer persecution" (2 Timothy 3:12). There is not a hero in the Bible who didn't have a counterpart fighting to keep the kingdom of God from advancing. And the greater your goal, the greater will be the opposition. Just remember that God is greater still.

4. *God promised to deliver Jeremiah from his obstacles.* The Lord said, "[Your enemies] shall not prevail against you. For I am with you . . . to deliver you" (Jeremiah 1:19). God's warning about obstacles would have been hollow without His promise to help Jeremiah overcome them. God didn't promise to get Jeremiah out of all his difficulties; rather, He promised to bring the prophet through them successfully.

We have the same comforting assurance in our struggles against difficulties in the life of passion. Jesus said, "In the world you will have tribulation; but be of good cheer, I have overcome the world" (John 16:33). That makes all the difference, doesn't it? When we pick up a favorite adventure movie, we know the hero will face all kinds of misfortunes—but we know that in the end he will triumph. Likewise, we know how our life comes out in the end. We know that God has assured a happy ending to this life for those of us who trust Him. We need only persevere and keep our eyes on the glory that He receives through all of it.

STOKE THE FIRE OR RETIRE?

Everyone who pursues a passion—for God, for family, for church, for self—will grow discouraged in the face of obstacles. There's no question Jeremiah did. In the face of the opposition he encountered, he likely wondered if his preaching was doing any good at all. In fact, we know he considered throwing in the towel and perhaps retiring to an old prophets' home.

In *The Message*, Eugene Peterson provided a contemporary version of Jeremiah's words in 20:7–8—probably the words that ran through his mind as he sat in the stocks in the temple gate, being pelted by rocks, rotten vegetables, and the rhetoric of rage from the community:

> You pushed me into this, God, and I let you do it.
> You were too much for me.
> And now I'm a public joke.
> They all poke fun at me.
> Every time I open my mouth
> I'm shouting, "Murder!" or "Rape!"
> And all I get for my God-warnings
> Are insults and contempt.

There you have it: Jeremiah's open confession—a twenty-five-hundred-year-old version of, "Do I really need this headache?" The New English Bible renders the next verse: "Sometimes I think, 'I will make no mention of his message. I will not speak as his messenger any more'" (v. 9).

On those days when everyone and everything seems to be working against your most passionate efforts, don't you sometimes think, *Who needs this?* If that thought doesn't cross your mind with some degree of regularity, then I question whether you are pursuing your passion after all.

Businesspeople talk about "opportunity costs." Opportunity costs are what a company incurs in missed revenues if it maintains its current course. For example, if XYZ Company chooses to manufacture and market product A instead of product B, they must figure in as a cost what they might have made by marketing product B instead.

All of us have opportunity costs in life. Every decision we make automatically excludes other options we might have pursued instead. And nowhere are opportunity costs greater than in the pursuit of a vision. Passionate people are often pioneers. They often labor alone and wait long, frustrating years to see any fruit. They often encounter opposition. Passionate people are the most likely of all to second-guess themselves, wondering, *What paths did I miss by going down this one?*

It will always be easier to go along to get along. But that's not what passionate people are about. Their goal is not acceptance; it's loyalty to their vision and call. Yes, there will be opportunities missed. And yes, some of those opportunities might have brought greater financial rewards, fewer headaches and backaches, and more companions along the way. Perhaps your passionate pursuits will produce those things anyway. But don't choose your path for those rewards. Choose the path you *can't not* choose.

Jeremiah didn't retire; he rekindled the sparks of that inner fire. In the face of opposition and the temptation to quit, he kept doing what he *couldn't not* do. Why? Because passion isn't about a comfortable life or big results; it's about following through with your conviction regardless of the cost. I'm not saying that results are unimportant. Passion is always directed at a goal, and the hope of reaching the goal continues to fuel our passion. But passion exists apart from reaching the goal. Passion exists because you believe what you are doing is right and righteous—and to deny your vision would be to deny who you are.

When I moved my family from a prospering ministry in the comfortable and familiar Midwest to a ministry with "challenges" in California, there were times when I found myself wondering, *Who needs this?* Since that time, when we would struggle to undertake something new or different or bigger, I sometimes flirted with the tantalizing notion of doing something else. But those moments never lasted long because I deeply believed God was in those moves and movements. The passion was ultimately for God Himself, and that meant I had to stand firm when I faced obstacles. To turn from my task would mean to turn from God. I had faith that God knew what He was doing in my life.

On Fire with Passion

As soon as Jeremiah uttered those words questioning the reasonableness of the pursuit of his passion, he snapped back to reality. He told himself:

> "I will not make mention of Him,
> Nor speak anymore in His name."
> But His word was in my heart like a burning fire
> Shut up in my bones;
> I was weary of holding it back,
> And I could not. (Jeremiah 20:9)

Jeremiah found the key! I'll say it as plainly as I can: Passion carries with it an obligation.

Oliver Wendell Holmes spoke in prophetlike terms when he wrote to a friend, "Life is a romantic business. It is painting a picture, not doing a sum—but you have to make the romance, and it will come to the question of how much fire you have in your belly."

Hebrews of Jeremiah's time didn't use the word *belly,* but the prophet had fire in his *bones.* That's as good a description of passion as I've heard. If you've ever burned to see something accomplished, you understand that phrase. Every part of you is tingling. Something has set you on fire!

Jeremiah felt that way, and it kept him from the temptation of closing shop in Jerusalem. He was going to stay the course. If God had waited since the foundation of creation to give him this job, then he could certainly hang in there and see it through. Again, the passion is ultimately for God Himself. If we understand that, and if we trust Him completely, there is nothing this world can do to stand in our way.

There is another sense in which passion presents an obligation. To make my point, I must turn to the words of philosopher Bertrand Russell. You should understand that Russell was an avowed atheist—no friend to the Christian faith. But all truth is God's truth, and I think the philosopher spoke truly when he said, "The opinions that are held with passion are always those for which no good ground exists; indeed the passion is the measure of the holder's lack of rational conviction. Opinions in politics and religion are almost always held passionately."

Here's why I think there is value in Russell's statement, despite his negative jab at religion. Whenever you say, "I *can't not* do this," you are admitting that your desires go beyond reason and logic. For Kiki Camarena, leaving a relatively safe job as a patrol officer for the dangerous world of confronting drug traffickers didn't make good sense. But passion is not about logic! Camarena felt obligated to make a difference in the lives of young people who were being ruined by the illicit drug trade over the Texas–Mexico border. He had to do something about it. He sensed an allegiance to a higher calling, something bigger and more significant than anything else he might do. It was the power behind his passion.

When Jeremiah felt the fire in his bones, he knew he would be facing the nation, but he had no option but to preach. It wasn't logical or reasonable, only *right*. He was being loyal to his God and to himself. So every time the hardhearted religious establishment knocked him down, he jumped back up and got in their faces. That fire was still burning, and you could almost see the smoke coming from the prophet's ears. He was aflame with God's message for people who were truth-impaired. Jeremiah realized that he was in this thing for the duration. Being a prophet is not a part-time job, and it offers no early retirement plans. All it offers are the truth and eternal rewards.

In forty years of ministry, I have observed that passion and security are not frequently found together. When I graduated from seminary, I accepted a position as a Christian education director and youth pastor in a large Baptist church in South Jersey. Donna and I loved our life. We poured ourselves into the young people who came to our Wednesday night Bible studies. We ran a Saturday basketball league for all the churches in the area. We had kids in our apartment from morning to night seven days a week, and we could feel the presence of God in our work.

I never thought of what I did as a job or as "going to work." This was our life—our passion. During this time I began to preach some at the church, and I realized that more than anything else, that was what I wanted to do with my life.

One day the phone rang in our little three-room apartment. The caller was a family friend who had begun a church-planting mission in Fort Wayne, Indiana. From his home church, he and his congregation had started eleven congregations, and they were ready now to start the twelfth. Would I be interested in becoming the new pastor of a church made up of seven families?

I knew I wanted to preach. But the part about starting a new church—that had not been anywhere in my calculations. I simply hadn't considered that possibility.

For two weeks Donna and I prayed. We had been at our current position for about two years. Our home and ministry were secure. Our comfort zone was comfortable. Moving to Fort Wayne, Indiana, would mean putting everything on the line.

I now realize this was one of the three most important decisions of my life. I struggled to make the right decision, and I told Donna I needed to get away for a day to think and pray about things. One of my favorite places at that time was the boardwalk in Ocean City, New Jersey. I knew I would be able to clear my head and think things through if I could just feel the ocean breeze and hear the waves crashing against the shore.

As it turned out, that day at Ocean City was a very cold one. After spending an hour or so walking up and down the boardwalk,

I stopped in a little café to get a cup of coffee and read the newspaper.

As I browsed the sports section of the *Philadelphia Inquirer,* I came across an article about legendary football coach Vince Lombardi. The article was written about Coach Lombardi's decision to leave his very successful Green Bay Packers job and go to coach one of the worst teams in the NFL.

The writer of the article asked the legendary coach why he would make such a move at this point in his career. His answer was printed in bold type in a box within the article: "I have discovered that there is more challenge in building than in maintaining."

When I read that statement, I knew what God wanted me to do. Those who know me will not laugh when I tell them that God used the sports page to direct my life. I could maintain the status quo. That would be the easy road to take. There was comfort and security in New Jersey. There was challenge and risk and potential failure in Fort Wayne. But something deep inside me hungered for the chance to trust God in an unfamiliar setting.

As you look out at the horizon that beckons you, you're likely to feel some of the same fear and insecurity I did. Welcome to the club! Passionate, visionary people spend their lives walking away from the easy route. What's ahead is uncertain, but nothing is more certain than the love and sovereignty of our Lord—and besides, excitement beckons over that horizon. You *can't not* do this, because it's what you were meant to do. You can feel it in your bones.

Part II

**LIFE
WIDE
OPEN**

Unleashing *the* Power
of a Passionate Life

Overcome the Enemies of the Passionate Life

T HERE IS NOTHING QUITE AS AWE-INSPIRING as a display of raw power. If you have witnessed any of the following, especially in person, you know what I'm talking about:

- With a deafening roar and a gush of flames, two rocket boosters release more than six million pounds of thrust, defying gravity and hurtling the space shuttle into orbit.

- Muscles rippling and hooves flying, a thoroughbred horse sprints away from the pack in the homestretch to win the Kentucky Derby by three lengths.

- A symphony orchestra charges through the pulse-pounding climax of Tchaikovsky's "1812 Overture," complete with cannon fire and a sky full of fireworks.

- The *whoosh* of Tiger Woods's mighty swing and the *crack* of the club head blast a little white ball 340 yards down the fairway.

- Tons of strategically placed explosives detonate with such precision that a forty-story skyscraper of concrete and steel is reduced to rubble in seconds.

Breathless at sights and sounds of power like this, all we can utter is, "Wow!"

But our awe is short-lived, isn't it? In less than two minutes, the flaming rocket boosters are spent and jettisoned. Crossing the finish line, the thoroughbred slows to a gallop then to a harmless trot. In mere seconds, Tiger's streaking golf ball dies in the air and falls to the ground. And once the condemned building collapses into a cloud of dust, the spectators go home. That's the way it is: Most explosions of power cannot be maintained indefinitely. Other forces at work, such as gravity, friction, limited capacity, fatigue, etc., eventually tame the outburst, quiet the thunder, and cool the flames.

Sir Isaac Newton, the famous seventeenth-century mathematician and physicist, discovered a law of motion that helps explain some of these realities. You probably learned Newton's first law of motion in your freshman science class. The second part of this law states: "An object in motion tends to stay in motion with the same speed and in the same direction unless acted upon by an unbalanced force."

In other words, Tiger Woods's golf ball would keep flying forever if it didn't encounter the forces of wind resistance, drag, and gravity. If it wasn't for fatigue, last year's Kentucky Derby champion might still be racing around the track and Lance Armstrong could race his bike through the Alps twenty-four hours a day. The point is this: There are a lot of forces at work that can diminish, dissipate, deflect, detour, discourage, or destroy unleashed power.

Any forward motion will encounter resistance—including your forward motion. There simply haven't been any great causes in history that didn't struggle against opposition. They wouldn't have been great movements otherwise.

But now is the time to take stock. We have looked inside ourselves and identified the fire in our bones. We know that God fashioned us, lovingly and from eternity, for a purpose. And just knowing that makes the fire burn more brightly, and it makes us hold our shoulders a little higher. But we also know we must be prepared for the struggles ahead. God has given us two promises: His presence and His power.

Now we feel the courage to go on. All the same, there is wisdom in knowing the enemy. In this section, we will come to know, if not love, the enemies of passion.

LIFE
UNLEASHING *the* POWER
WIDE
of a PASSIONATE LIFE
OPEN

When the Fire Goes Out

KILLER DANA was the most notorious wave in California. When it was really ripping and roaring, the best surfers in the world gave it plenty of distance. Legendary surfers with names like George "Peanuts" Larson and Jim "Burrhead" Drever knew that given the traditional techniques of their sport, that wave was more than they could handle.

Then came a teenager to prove them wrong.

In 1953, a boy named Phil Edwards paddled out toward Killer Dana beside the best surfers in the business, and people gasped. Was this kid crazy? He wouldn't last three minutes against the toughest wave the West Coast had to offer.

But Edwards came right at Killer Dana behind Burrhead Drever and shocked the rest of his party of surfers by cutting back into the foam. The rest of the surfers were riding their boards back to the shore—after all, that's how it was usually done. But Edwards challenged the wave with a style and artistry that gave birth to a whole new sport: performance surfing. He quickly became the great superstar of the sport, just at the time when surfing came into its own in the popular imagination through movies, Beach Boys songs, and California culture.

Edwards was unimpressed with the crowds. "There are

uncounted millions of people who now go through life without any sort of real, vibrant kick," he said. He gave these people a name: "the legions of the unjazzed."

He was talking about people who live their entire life without taking risks. "There is a need in all of us for controlled danger," said the surfboard philosopher. Edwards believed that life is lived out where the foam is breaking, out where it's easy to take a tumble and get a mouthful of salt water. In his lingo, to face that kind of excitement is to "be jazzed." Even the best practitioners of his sport, in his view, were taking it easy, avoiding the risks.[1]

The passionate life is about playing to our potential—giving it the best shot we have, even when the odds are against us, even when we're weary, even when nobody else advises it. Passion pushes us forward as it did Phil Edwards. Athletes call this kind of effort "leaving it all on the field." But as we all know, sometimes a team doesn't play to its potential. Sometimes an army doesn't give its best fight. Sometimes we are all numbered among the legions of the unjazzed.

I'm talking about the sinister cancer of passivity, which slowly but inexorably squeezes the passion out of our life. I'm talking about how the adventure, excitement, and fulfillment we all crave is smothered by the wet blanket of apathy, indifference, and stoicism. The passionate life is one of activity, enthusiasm, and energy. Passivity shorts out all the circuits and leaves us bored and in a rut. Ferdinand Foch, marshal of France at the turn of the twentieth century, said, "The most powerful weapon on earth is the human soul on fire." Passivity snuffs out that vital inner blaze.

Passivity doesn't only attack our spiritual life. It is just as easy to slip into a passive lifestyle in our relationships with family and friends, in our work, in our activities and ministries at church, and in our extracurricular activities. In fact, if these other areas of our life are marked by apathy, boredom, and a *Who cares?* attitude, it's a sure bet that the vitality of our relationship to Christ has dwindled to a simmer. Unleashing the power of a passionate life begins by defeating the passivity in our heart toward God.

In the book of Revelation, Jesus spoke pointedly to two groups of Christians whose once-fiery passion for God and for life in general had cooled to a mundane and ineffective existence. I believe the churches of Ephesus and Laodicea demonstrate two stages many of today's churches and individual Christians go through in the decline from passion to passivity. Examining the experiences of these New Testament churches and listening closely to Christ's message to each of them can help us keep the fires of passion burning brightly in our own heart.

A DYING FLAME

In the first century, Ephesus was the most prominent city in the Roman province of Asia. The city held one of the Seven Wonders of the World: the Temple of Artemis, a magnificent structure built in honor of the Roman goddess of fertility. But by the end of the first century when the book of Revelation was written, Ephesus was in decline. It was a city living on its laurels, trying to maintain the glory of its past. The harbor was filling with silt, causing commerce to decline. And new religions, Christianity among them, were competing for the attention of its citizens. Ephesus was a city whose passion had flickered and died.

The church followed the city's lead. The flaming fellowship was now reduced to dying embers. Where does the passion go when it all leaks out?

We can't say that the church at Ephesus lacked *dedication.* Jesus opened His message to them with these words: "I know your works, your labor" (Revelation 2:2). They were active and busy, and Jesus commended them for it. The word *labor* implies working to the point of exhaustion. There were apparently many in the church who were so busy in the service of the church that they were worn out. They were dedicated to building the church in Ephesus and making an impact on the city.

Nor was there a problem with a lack of *determination.* Jesus also commended them for their patience in service (v. 2) and in suffering (v. 3). Acts 19 tells about the persecution that came upon the believers in Ephesus from those who rose up against them. The silversmiths union, which profited from selling silver statues of the goddess Diana, was not happy with the anti-idolatry message of the Christians. The clash escalated into a riot. But the Christians there persevered in their determination to make a difference.

This kind of determination in suffering reminds me of a wonderful statement by the great nineteenth-century London preacher, Charles Spurgeon:

> Pray God to send a few more men with what the Americans call "grit" in them; men, who when they know a thing to be right, will not turn away, or turn aside, or stop; men who will persevere all the more because there are difficulties to meet or foes to encounter; who stand all the more true to their Master because they are opposed; who, the more they are thrust into the fire, the hotter they become, who just like the bow, the further the string is drawn, the more powerfully it sends forth arrows, and so the more they are trodden upon, the more mighty they become in the cause of truth against error.[2]

Determination to hang in there seems to have been present in the Ephesian church.

We also know that the problem in the church at Ephesus wasn't a lack of *discipline* or *discernment*. In fact, the twenty-first-century church would do well to imitate the church discipline practiced by the Ephesian believers. They did not allow evil to spring up in their midst and bear fruit, and Jesus commended them for their discipline. They "tested those who say they are apostles and are not, and have found them liars" (v. 3). It was not uncommon for apostle wanna-bes to circulate through first-century churches, looking for hospitality and a place to exercise their self-appointed authority. This church grilled the visitors on their theology and practice and sent them packing if they didn't measure up.

So what was the problem at Ephesus? Today, if we described a church as dedicated, determined, discerning, and disciplined, we would be talking about a church of some notoriety. And that's the root of the problem. Despite all the Ephesian Christians had going for them, Jesus said, "Nevertheless I have this against you, that you have left your first love" (v. 4). In less than a century, the church at Ephesus had moved from faith to formalism. In all their busyness they had lost their passion for Jesus. They were so involved in keeping up the religious practices of the church that they had become passive in their devotion to the Head of the church.

I see the same thing happening today. There are nearly four hundred thousand churches dotting the landscape of America, but what effect are we having? We are making an impact to some degree; I would hate to imagine what America would look and act like if the church were not here. But are we having the level of impact we could? Are we turning our society upside down the way Jesus and the apostles did theirs? I don't think so. And in my view, it's because we are more in love with the church than with the Lord of the church. We have moved from faith to formalism. We have lost our first love.

Losing our first love is another way of saying we have lost our passion. And the way the church at large—or any local church like yours or mine—loses its passion is by individual Christians becoming passive about devotion to Christ. Life wide open is not about doing great things for God apart from knowing and loving God intimately. You can serve tirelessly on every committee in the church and faithfully attend every function of the church—even workdays! But without the fire of passion for Jesus burning within you, you won't accomplish much more than the space shuttle under butane power. We must say with St. John of the Cross:

> Forever at this door
> I gave my heart and soul.
> My fortune too.

I've no flock anymore,
No other work in view.
My occupation: love.
It's all I do.

FORMALISM IS FAILURE

Let me state the problem with the church in Laodicea up-front: When God finds apostasy in the church, He is unhappy. But when God finds passivity in the church, He is angry. Passivity is unacceptable.

Laodicea was perhaps the wealthiest city in the Roman province of Asia Minor in the first century. The money had gone to their head and dampened their heart. The church had once been soulful, passionate, and wide open. Paul mentioned the Laodicean believers several times in his letter to the church at Colossae, encouraging the Colossians to share his letter with the church at Laodicea (see Colossians 4:12–16).

Despite Laodicea's material prosperity, the city lacked one important thing: an adequate water supply. They had to run a pipeline from nearby Hierapolis to obtain hot water from the mineral hot springs, and they piped in cold water from the springs in neighboring Colossae. But since the pipelines were built above ground and not insulated, the water the Laodiceans received was neither fully hot nor fully cold, but lukewarm.

Hot mineral water is good for bathing and gargling. Cool spring water is good for quenching a blazing thirst. But lukewarm water is neither refreshing nor therapeutic. The lukewarm water of Laodicea became a picture of the passive faith of the church there. Jesus said, "You're not cold, you're not hot—far better to be either cold or hot! You're stale. You're stagnant. You make me want to vomit" (Revelation 3:16 MSG).

Jesus had three problems with the church at Laodicea, all of which grew out of its lack of passion for Christ.

1. *The Laodicean church had compromised its faith* (see Revelation 3:15–16). The Christian life is supposed to be hot, passionate, and fervent—not tepid. Apollos taught the Scriptures in Ephesus with great energy and excitement (see Acts 18:25). The word used in that verse is *fervent,* defined as "showing passionate enthusiasm" or "glowingly hot." Paul urged us to be "fervent in spirit, serving the Lord" (Romans 12:11). James called us to "effective, fervent prayer" (James 5:16). And Peter stated that we are to have "fervent love for one another" (1 Peter 4:8). Does your faith have passionate enthusiasm? Is it glowingly hot?

2. *The Laodicean church was conceited.* This church boasted, "I am rich, have become wealthy, and have need of nothing" (Revelation 3:17). Jesus disagreed, stating that the church was oblivious to being "wretched, miserable, poor, blind, and naked" (v. 17). Conceit can't see the faults in its own character, but Jesus can see them. Laodicea was wealthy, but the church was spiritually destitute. The city boasted of its textile business, but the church was spiritually naked. And though Laodicea was famous for its eye medicine, the church was blind.

3. *The Laodicean church was Christless* (see Revelation 3:20). They were so focused on themselves and their so-called success that they didn't notice who was missing from the assembly: Jesus. To spiritually lukewarm believers, it doesn't matter if Jesus is present or not. They become so caught up with themselves and busy with their agenda that they carry on without Him. And when Jesus does come near, they won't let Him warm their tepid hearts.

Passion for God and his kingdom must move from something we occasionally think about to something we embrace heart and soul. Sue Monk Kidd writes: "I'm discovering that a spiritual journey is a lot like a poem. You don't merely recite a poem or analyze it intellectually. You dance it, sing it, cry it, feel it on your skin and in your bones. You move with it and feel its caress. It falls on you like a teardrop or wraps around you like a smile. It lives in the heart and the body as well as the spirit and the head."[3]

Churches fall into spiritual passivity the same way they lose their passion: one careless believer at a time. If the church today—yours and mine in particular—is going to be a passionate influence on our needy world, it will only happen as individual Christians like you and me throw off the conceit of this age and pursue wholeheartedly an intimate, passionate relationship with Jesus.

FROM PASSIVITY TO PASSION

While in London to attend a conference, my wife, Donna, and I visited a number of the famous churches in the city. One of the most famous is St. Paul's Cathedral, designed by renowned British architect Sir Christopher Wren. St. Paul's is also the home of a large painting by artist Holman Hunt that is known the world over.

This marvelous painting features the front of a neglected cottage. Thistles have grown up the front wall and grass covers the entry walk. Vines, weeds, and rusty hinges in the painting convey a sense that nobody cares about the cottage or its residents. The scene represents a neglected life, a heart where passion has long since cooled.

But standing at the door of this cottage is the kind King, Jesus Christ, holding a lantern from which the painting derives its title, "The Light of the World." The lantern light casts a warm glow over the front of the run-down home. And with His upraised right hand, Christ is knocking on the door.

It is a painting of stark contrasts. King Jesus, resplendent in royal robes, bathed in the light of His own glory, seeks admittance to this humble home. The most intriguing aspect of the painting is the fact that there is no latch on Jesus's side of the door. An early viewer of the painting approached the artist to point out the "mistake" of forgetting to put a latch on the door. Holman's reply reflects the key to Christ's gaining entrance to our lives: "No, it is not a mistake. The handle is on the inside. Only we can open the door and allow Christ to come in."

How often I have seen Christians whose lives are represented by the neglected cottage in Holman Hunt's famous painting. Where the fire of passion once filled the windows with the light of vibrant life, now only the dimness of passivity is evident. Once the pathway was packed firm and the grounds weeded and trimmed for the frequent, welcomed visitor, but now the threshold is rarely crossed. And the door that was always ajar in anticipation of the Master's fellowship is now shut and locked from the inside against a friend who is now regarded as a stranger.

Jesus said, "Behold, I stand at the door and knock. If anyone hears My voice and opens the door, I will come in to him and dine with him, and he with Me" (Revelation 3:20). The key to unlocking the door to passion in your life, not just for spiritual things but for every facet of life, is throwing open the door of your life to Jesus and inviting Him to enter. It is impossible to be passive in the presence of Passion Personified!

If the vines of passivity are creeping up the walls of your life, if the path to your door is nearly impassable, if Jesus's knock at your heart's door has gone unanswered in recent days, I beg you to throw off your passivity. Open yourself once again so that passion rules. Allow the Light of the world to so fill your life that His warmth and brilliance flows out to others in darkness. A. W. Tozer said, "Keep your feet on the ground, but let your heart soar as high as it will. Refuse to be average or to surrender to the chill of your spiritual environment."

If you have surrendered to passivity by allowing your passion for God and life to become lukewarm, you must heed the call Jesus issued to both the Ephesian and Laodicean churches: "Repent!" (Revelation 2:5; 3:19).

"Isn't that something for non-Christians to do?" you may ask. Yes, and if you are still investigating the Christian life, you no doubt sense Christ gently knocking at the door of your life. He wants you to change your mind about Him by surrendering to His lordship. But repentance is also something for Christians to do when the flame of passion inside has dwindled to a flicker or gone out.

Repent. Change your mind. Don't lock passion or the Passion Giver out of your life any longer. That door handle is on your side, and no one can fling the door wide open but you—just as no one can give you a life wide open but Jesus. He stands at the door and knocks . . . and knocks . . . and knocks.

9

LIFE
UNLEASHING *the* POWER
WIDE
of a PASSIONATE LIFE
OPEN

Frozen By Feeble Faith

WALTER INVITED HIS GOOD FRIEND Arthur to take a ride with him out into the country. They drove past groves of fruit trees and dilapidated shacks to an area that looked to Arthur like a barren wasteland. Walter began telling his friend about the exciting plans he had for this boring parcel of land southeast of downtown Los Angeles, California. Walter's express purpose was to give Arthur the opportunity to become an investor in his dream.

Walter had enough money for his main project, but he wanted to ensure that the land surrounding his venture would be bought up at the same time. He was confident that within five years the whole area would be filled with hotels, restaurants, and even a convention center serving the throngs of people who came to visit his development.

But Walter's friend, radio and television personality Art Linkletter, could not see the potential and turned down the opportunity to buy up the acres and acres of land that now surround Disneyland, the dream of his friend, Walt Disney. Today that "barren wasteland" in Orange County, California, is worth billions of dollars.

How would you feel if you were Art Linkletter? While open doors of opportunity that size come along rarely, if ever, for people like you and me, there are many smaller doors of opportunity that are presented to us on a daily basis. God constantly invites us to trust Him and experience ever-expanding dimensions of His faith-fulness and blessing. But far too often we are like the hesitant Linkletter. We hang back, not sure of what we should do. Or we walk away from the open door altogether. We allow fear and feeble faith to quench the fire of passion for a project, a product, or a plan God has put in our heart.

Why do we so often freeze up on the threshold of a God-given opportunity? Many Christians fail to walk through God's open doors because of a faulty view of God. We see Him as incapable of taking care of us in a new and possibly risky venture. Or we fear that, once we walk through the open door, He will slam it behind us and leave us to fend for ourselves. We often cannot step out because our faith in God is feeble. If we had a childlike, trusting attitude toward our heavenly Father, we would walk confidently through the door He holds open for us.

It's all an issue of trust, isn't it? "In God We Trust" may be engraved on your coins, but is it engraved upon your heart? When the big decisions really come down to the moment of truth, do you really believe God will care for you?

You may remember what Jesus observed about His own home-town, Nazareth. Mark 6:5–6 tells us, "He could do no mighty work there, except that He laid His hands on a few sick people and healed them. And He marveled because of their unbelief." I wonder how many people could have the same thing said about them: "He could do no mighty work in his/her life."

God forbid that Jesus Christ should marvel at my unbelief or yours. Imagine how He must feel because He is the opener and closer of all doors. He is the creator of every opportunity and the master of every mission. When He opens a door, we need only walk through. But I'm like you; I hesitate for a moment. After all, it's *dark* on the other side. We don't know what lies in there!

Living with passion requires us to walk by faith—to go to the edge of all the light that we have and take *one more step*. God gives me the only the briefest, dimmest glimpse of what lies over the threshold. He smiles because He knows that this next step, this hard step, will be a real character builder—a faith investment. The next time I step through an open door, I'll have an ounce more faith.

PASSIONATE PEOPLE LOOK FOR GOD'S OPEN DOORS

The apostle John wrote from his exile on the Isle of Patmos to the church of Philadelphia. He encouraged that church and us with these words: "These things says He who is holy, He who is true, He who has the key of David, He who opens and no one shuts, and shuts and no one opens: 'I know your works. See, I have set before you an open door, and no one can shut it; for you have a little strength, have kept My word, and have not denied My name'" (Revelation 3:7–8).

John is giving Christ's words to the church at Philadelphia, and he says that Christ has set an open door before them. I can't imagine anything more exciting than the promise of new opportunity as a gift from the Lord Himself. I would like to think that Jesus has this message for every church on the face of the earth: "I have set before you an open door."

Yet we all know that most churches are filled with people who aren't eager to walk through any door other than the one leading to the parking lot. Why are there so many people who fail to burn with excitement about the idea of newness and growth? I've watched Christians face this issue for many years, and I've come up with four observations.

1. *God's open doors are often disguised as problems.* It was the brilliant cartoon philosopher Pogo who once observed, "Gentlemen, we are surrounded by insurmountable opportunities." What we are certain are obstacles to our exploits for God—lack of money, machinery, methodology, or manpower—are often God's opportunities in disguise. One person's stumbling block is another's stepping-stone.

A few years ago our church had grown so large that we

couldn't contain the crowd. We were already meeting in three different locations. We needed to radically expand the facilities on our main campus so everyone could meet together. We faced challenges that seemed hopeless. For several years we couldn't agree, and we were at an impasse.

Eventually we began to look at our problem and see an opportunity. While we were stuck in a no-building mode, the Lord showed us another way to reach even more people than if we had huge new facilities. We began Turning Point Ministries, which now sends the gospel over radio, television, and in print. And yes, eventually we expanded our facilities as well. But if we had not been stuck with the building "problem," we may never have seen God's open doors for radio and television ministry.

2. *God's open doors are often time-sensitive.* An Arabic proverb says that the dawn does not come twice to awaken a person. When Walt Disney was planning Disneyland, he offered Art Linkletter an opportunity to buy land surrounding the site—land he knew would dramatically increase in value. Disney needed an answer quickly, but Linkletter balked, and the door to untold wealth quickly slammed shut.

Passionate, faith-filled people are prompt to act on opportunities. If you fail to walk through a door God has opened, it doesn't mean He is finished with you. But if you don't step up in a timely manner, He will likely turn to someone who will not hesitate.

When Jewish leaders failed to accept Jesus as their long-awaited Messiah, God's door of opportunity closed. Jesus said to them, "The kingdom of God will be taken from you and given to a nation bearing the fruits of it" (Matthew 21:43). God turned to the Gentiles with the gospel. Israel will yet have an opportunity to embrace Jesus, but only after many centuries of regret for having missed their first opportunity (see Zechariah 12:10). When God presents you with a door of opportunity, don't hesitate to step out in faith.

3. *When we start through God's open doors, we are often met by resistance.* Have you ever gotten caught in a revolving door? Few

moments are more comedic—getting halfway through and deciding you don't want to enter the building after all. Sometimes we try to back out of God's doorways. We think, *I must not have heard God correctly. I wouldn't be experiencing opposition if God had opened this door.* But if the apostle Paul anticipated opposition when approaching God's open doors, we should too. He wrote, "I will tarry in Ephesus until Pentecost. For a great and effective door has opened to me, and there are many adversaries" (1 Corinthians 16:8–9).

The opposition of trials, temptations, tribulations, or testy people is not a sign that you're entering the wrong door. In most cases it's a sign that you're exactly where God wants you. No worthwhile attempt will ever go unchallenged. Opportunity and opposition are natural counterparts.

4. *Open doors are often missed because of fear.* I can't think of one opportunity God has opened to me that I did not reach for with trembling hands. Why? Because all open doors lead into the future—whether in five minutes, five days, or five years. And since the future is unknown to us, we are often fearful to step out in faith. We defeat our fear of the unknown by learning more about God, who has made Himself knowable. He has not given us a spirit of fear, but He has promised to go with us wherever we go in His will. You can walk boldly into the future when you know that the God of the future goes with you.

Is there an opportunity in front of you at this very moment that has left you nervous, scared, weak, and faithless? Wonderful! You may be looking at a door God has opened for you. Take His hand, trust His promises, and step over the threshold. Every step of faith you take toward God will also take you one step away from your crippling fear.

PASSIONATE PEOPLE WALK THROUGH GOD'S OPEN DOORS

In 1777, it became clear to the Continental Congress that an alliance with France was America's only defense against England.

But who should be sent to the French court to strike a deal? The obvious choice was John Adams, the scholar-lawyer who had played a pivotal role in shaping the Declaration of Independence. But would Adams consent to further sacrifice? He had already spent the better part of four years in Philadelphia, away from his family in Massachusetts, helping to forge the fundamentals of the new American government.

When considering whether to accept the appointment, John and Abigail Adams reached a turning point in their lives. Neither of them wanted the appointment that would separate them for a year and a half. But they decided that John must go to France or all that had been accomplished in America's fight for independence might be lost. It was a decision to walk through a door of opportunity at great personal cost. Eighteen months after departing, John Adams returned to Massachusetts, having forged an alliance that led to an American victory in the Revolution. He would later serve his country as its second president.

What if John Adams had said, "Enough! I have sacrificed more than my fair share already. Let someone else walk through this open door"? Fortunately, we will never know, because he said the opposite. He believed that God had placed before America an opportunity that must be grasped. America stands independent today in no small part because a weary revolutionary named John Adams recognized a watershed moment for what it was—an opportunity to change the world.

Stepping through God's open doors leads to changed lives. As Christians, we will find doors of opportunity opening before us every day. The question is, Do we have the courage and passion to walk through them? Let's agree on this: Any door God opens for you is a door you can and should walk through. Here are four considerations that will help set your faith and spiritual feet in motion.

1. *Your faithful response to God's opportunities will pay dividends in time and eternity.* John Adams and the rest of America's founding fathers had the taste of destiny on their lips. They knew

that they were involved in a once-in-a-lifetime venture; nations are not birthed every day. Because Adams was a strong believer in the providential hand of God being active in the founding of the new nation, he weighed his personal sacrifices not only in light of America's future but in light of eternity. He sensed that something more important than today's immediate gains was at stake. A country where citizens could live free from tyranny and oppression was to be valued above all other considerations.

It will cost you to walk through God's open doors. At the very least, you will give up the security and comfort of the familiar—and usually more. But no harvest is reaped without first sacrificing a seed. Only when we learn to view life through the lens of the long view, even the eternal view, will we see that the sacrifices of this world are nothing in light of what is gained by going through God's open doors. You may need to pay a price now to help a friend endure a crisis, find shelter for a homeless person, adopt an orphan, or any number of passionate ministries to Jesus and others, but think of the eternal dividends! Passionate, faith-filled people recognize that they must sow in order to reap, and they willingly release possessions, comfort, and security in order to gain the blessings of tomorrow.

2. *It will cost you and others dearly if you fail to grasp God's opportunities.* You and I pay for our groceries in U.S. dollars instead of British pounds today because John Adams sailed through the door that opened before him. Adams struck a deal with France, and it was France's aid against the British that bought time for our developing nation to muster its own defenses. Had Adams not acted, who knows how different our history might have been or how our national and personal freedoms may have been affected?

Just as you cannot estimate the positive outcome from passionately embracing God's opportunities, neither can you guess what you and others will miss when feeble faith freezes you at the threshold. For example, you would never intentionally withhold food from your spouse or children; they would starve to death. But think of what happens to them emotionally and spiritually when you are more involved in your work or a hobby than in the lives of your dearest ones. Believe me, it's a price you don't want to pay.

3. *Your faithful response to God's opportunities will be aided by those who encourage and support you.* John and Abigail Adams mutually supported one another. Adams's wife was every bit his equal in intellect and passion when it came to the trials and tribulations associated with founding the new republic. Their lengthy correspondence during Adams's many absences from home fills volumes of thoughtful, spiritual, respectful, and passionate prose. David McCullough, Pulitzer Prize-winning biographer of John Adams, spoke highly of Abigail Adams and regretted that she has not received the credit due her for her husband's success as a founding father. Who knows how John Adams's contribution might have been limited had he not enjoyed his wife's encouragement and support?

It would take another chapter in this book to recount all the occasions God has used my passionate life partner, Donna, to jump-start me at the threshold of one of God's open doors. Sometimes our spouse brings to decision-making an objectivity and a "features-and-benefits analysis" that we can't see. While we're staring at the trees, they are surveying the forest, assessing the bigger picture.

We more readily act upon our passion when we surround ourselves with people of like passion. You need a team of supporters and encouragers on your side, such as your spouse and children, a Bible study or fellowship group, prayer partners, accountability partners, spiritual mentors, and counselors. These individuals cannot act on the opportunities God has set out before you; that's your job. But they can supply counsel, instruction, encouragement, comfort, and even correction to help you follow through with what God has given you to do.

4. *Walking through God's open doors will serve as an example to others.* When John Adams set off for France in 1777, he took with him his ten-year-old son, John Quincy, who would later

become the sixth president of the United States. By all comparisons, John Quincy Adams was his father's superior when it came to learning and political and international leadership. His education in Europe's schools, both on this trip and during return visits to the Continent, moved him far ahead of his American peers. He learned several languages and became familiar with court etiquette. The younger Adams was even sent to Russia as an American delegate to the royal court—at age fifteen!

What if John Adams had not walked through the open door to France? We don't know what the negative impact might have been on his son, John Quincy Adams. But history does reveal the positive impact of his father's example. John Quincy equaled and perhaps even exceeded his father's passion and patriotism.

Who is watching when you contemplate the open doors God places before you? Who is learning from your example as you express either feeble or passionate faith? Your spouse, your children, and your closest friends, to be sure. But there are doubtless many others of whom you may not be aware. A new Christian who is looking to you as a role model to follow. A Christian friend who is paralyzed by fear. A coworker or neighbor who has never learned to trust God. The apostle Paul did not hesitate to say, "Imitate me, just as I also imitate Christ" (1 Corinthians 11:1). This was not a statement of self-promotion; it was the confident assertion of one who knew the will of God and was passionate about doing it. Can you make a similar, bold claim?

FREEZING FEAR OR FEEBLE FAITH?

Two closely related enemies meet us at the threshold of passionate living: freezing fear and feeble faith. People of passion respond by being alert to these opportunities and trusting God as they walk through them with boldness. These doors can appear in any area of our daily life. They may take the form of opportunities for continuing education, advancement at work, developing new skills, or meeting new people. They may come as opportunities for greater levels of Christian ministry: a deeper personal commitment to Christ, a new mentoring relationship, greater leadership responsibility, or increased obedience in financial stewardship. Or they may appear as opportunities for family growth: taking a class together, going on a mission trip together, or setting new priorities for family finances.

Watch for newly opening doors. God's work is accomplished in this world through them. Don't allow feeble faith to leave you standing on the doorstep. Be a person of passion who not only sees God's opportunities but charges through them with faith in His provision.

As I look back over my life, I realize that I have experienced a series of open doors that all go back to one particular door God opened during my college days.

I was a speech major in college and had dreams of a career as a radio broadcaster. I was working at two different radio stations and was learning everything I could about the industry. I was certain that this was God's will for my life—that is, until one day a few months before graduation.

My father, who was the president of the college I attended, called me into his office and asked me if I would help him over the weekend. He said that he had scheduled all of the faculty members' student preachers for the weekend, and he needed someone to go to a little church near Columbus, Ohio, to speak to a congregation of about thirty-five farm people. He said, "David, I think you can do this. It would be a great blessing to those folks and a real help to me."

At first I thought he was joking, but I realized as we continued our conversation that he was dead serious. After offering some rather feeble excuses, I agreed to go. I asked my fiancée, who is now my wife, to go with me, and she agreed.

When we arrived at Fairfield Baptist Church in Thurston, Ohio, I realized that my father had accurately communicated to us the nature of the church. It was a small country church with about thirty-five people in attendance.

I gave my testimony in the morning service and shared a couple of verses of Scripture. After we had greeted the people, one of the families of the church invited us to stay and have dinner with them. We accepted the invitation and were enjoying our time at the dinner table until the father happened to mention that they were looking forward to my speaking in the evening service.

My father had conveniently forgotten to mention that I was to stay for the evening service. Worse than that, I had just unloaded everything I knew in the morning service. I spent the afternoon reviewing what I'd said earlier. Then I simply repackaged it with a few new thoughts and presented the results to them that night.

As we were leaving the church, they asked us if we would come back the next week. After giving them a variation on a rerun, that was the first miracle. Then I heard myself replying, "Yes, of course we will." That was the second miracle.

The greatest miracle of all was how God used that experience to open the door to my becoming a preacher of the gospel. He calls us in many different ways—we never know how or when. An elder businessman once confided to his son, "The secret is to jump at every opportunity." The son asked how he could know when an opportunity was coming. The father replied, "You can't—you just have to keep jumping!"

The little church of thirty-five members kept me jumping, but in the end I had leaped into a new, God-given calling. All I had to do was say yes when my father asked me to preach for a day, then yes again when my Father asked me to preach for a lifetime.

May your open doors be just as delightful and rewarding.

LIFE
UNLEASHING *the* POWER
WIDE
of a PASSIONATE LIFE
OPEN

Me? No Way!

ED NERVOUSLY PACED THE CROWDED SIDEWALK outside
Holton's Shoe Store in downtown Boston. His brief lunch hour
was nearly over, but he had not yet done what he had come to do.
Inside the shoe store was an eighteen-year-old clerk who was a
member of the Sunday school class Ed taught at church. The young
man had seemed bored in class and generally disinterested in spiritual things since he began attending church one year earlier. Ed felt
burdened to talk to him about his relationship with Christ, and
today was the day he had planned to do so. But he was nervous
about it. *What if he won't listen to me? What if he thinks I'm being
too pushy and quits the class all together? What if he gets angry and
throws me out?*

Breathing a prayer for courage, Ed finally walked into the store
and found the clerk busy at work. The young man was surprised to
see his Sunday school teacher, but Ed quickly got to the point. "I
came to tell you how much Christ loves you," he said. They talked
for several minutes, then the young man knelt down on the spot
and opened his life to Jesus Christ. Later the clerk related the
impact of his conversion: "I was in a new world. The birds sang
sweeter, the sun shone brighter. I'd never known such peace."

Ed left the shoe store that day rejoicing that he had overcome his self-doubt and fear and let God use him to share the good news with the young shoe clerk. This fearful Sunday school teacher could not have imagined that, during the next 150 years, millions of people would be just as thankful that he had overcome his anxiety and hesitation that April day in 1855 to share the gospel in a shoe store. Though unaware until now, you may be one of the people whose spiritual journey was influenced by this Sunday school teacher, Edward Kimball.

You see, the eighteen-year-old Boston shoe clerk Kimball talked to that day was Dwight L. Moody, who became one of America's great evangelists in the latter half of the nineteenth century. Moody had an impact all over the world. In addition, Moody later counseled a young man named J. Wilbur Chapman on the assurance of his salvation. Chapman became a Presbyterian minister, evangelist, and Moody's friend and colleague in ministry. Moody and Chapman strongly influenced a young professional baseball player named Billy Sunday, whom God also called to evangelistic ministry. It is estimated that three hundred thousand men and women came to faith in Christ during Billy Sunday's two hundred campaigns.

But Kimball's legacy didn't stop there. A 1924 Billy Sunday evangelistic campaign in Charlotte, North Carolina, resulted in the formation of the Charlotte Businessman's Club, which continued to evangelize the region. In 1934, the CBMC invited evangelist Mordecai Ham to conduct a campaign in Charlotte. A young man of eighteen reluctantly attended one of those meetings and then gave his life to Christ. His name was Billy Graham. No one has preached the gospel to more people than Billy Graham.

Was Billy Graham instrumental in your coming to Christ? If not directly, perhaps the person who brought you to Christ was influenced by his preaching. At the very least, you likely know someone who became a Christian because of this great evangelist's ministry.

The gripping reality is this: Countless millions of people have been brought to faith in Christ through the preaching of D. L. Moody, Billy Sunday, and Billy Graham during the past century and a half. What would have happened if a Sunday school teacher named Edward Kimball had allowed self-doubt to detour him from living out his passion for sharing Christ with others?

Another significant enemy of the life of passion is self-doubt—the inner, gnawing sense that you are unqualified or incapable of making a difference in your world. You may say something like, "Why should I work so hard at pursuing a passionate life? I'm nobody special. I can't do much. Passionate people have it all together, and that's not me."

Had Edward Kimball taken that attitude, he may never have entered the shoe store. And if you allow self-doubt to corner you, you will not only rob yourself of the exciting life of passion God has for you, but you will also rob others of God's influence through you.

The Nobility of Being a Nobody

Where does self-doubt come from? I believe we begin to question our usefulness to God when we compare ourselves to others who seem more gifted or competent. You and I live in a superstar-saturated society, and that phenomenon seeps into the church. Everywhere we turn we are confronted by the images of Christians who are professional athletes, movie stars, and other celebrities. We're delighted to know that people with so much fame would give their life to Christ. But we're still conveying a subtle message that people with fame are the only ones who count—and therefore, God surely doesn't need us ordinary types if he has NBA basketball stars or cinema icons.

Leighton Ford was speaking at an open-air crusade in Halifax, Nova Scotia. Billy Graham would be following him to the microphone on the next night, and he'd arrived a day early. Billy came incognito and sat on the grass at the rear of the crowd. No one recognized him in his hat and dark glasses. Directly in front of him sat an elderly gentleman who seemed to be listening intently. When Leighton Ford invited people to come forward as an open sign of commitment, Billy decided to do a little personal evangelism. He tapped the man on the shoulder and asked, "Would you like to accept Christ? I'll be glad to walk down the aisle with you if you want to."

The old man looked him up and down, thought for a moment, and then said, "Naw, I think I'll just wait till the big gun comes tomorrow night."[1] The irony, of course, is that if there were such a thing as "big guns" in the kingdom of God, this man was missing his big chance. But the underlying point that should sadden us is that a big-gun mentality had spread even into as holy a moment as a faith commitment. We are coming into the presence of Christ Himself! Who needs "guns" any bigger than that?

The phenomenon stretches to lower levels too. Your pastor may not be a superstar, but he may be such a dynamic speaker that you discount your own ability to communicate the gospel. At work, your boss has an MBA, so you think too little of your own potential. You feel you can't teach Sunday school because of the master teacher down the hall. You feel you can't lead a neighborhood group because someone else is more experienced—and on and on it goes.

Many of us, as children, were the last to be selected when the team captain was choosing players for kickball. From that experience onward, we knew how badly it stung to be reminded of our failings. Then we had a crush on that popular kid in high school who rejected us and broke our heart. We resolved never to feel that pain again. It was easier to accept a low view of ourselves and to set our goals as low as possible.

What we didn't realize was the fact that a lifetime of self-doubt is far more painful and damaging than shooting for the stars and falling short. Being occasionally picked last is less painful than never having a team identity. Being romantically rejected is less hurtful than never finding love at all.

Besides, where is it written that one must be famous, spectacularly talented, or radiantly beautiful to lead a passionate, effective life? Think about the disciples of Jesus. Were they famous for their accomplishments before Jesus called them and used them? No, before they met Christ they were basically nobodies: peasants, fishermen, and a despised tax collector. They were citizens of the smallest geographical area of the known world at that time, yet Jesus selected them and empowered them to take His gospel around the globe.

When God chooses someone to live and work passionately for Him, He doesn't just select society's elite. First Corinthians 1:26 states, "For you see your calling, brethren, that not many wise according to the flesh, not many mighty, not many noble, are called." It may surprise you—and even liberate you—to realize that God does not enlist the majority of His servants from the ranks of the wise, the mighty, the noble, or the beautiful. Martin Luther was an obscure monk, stricken by low confidence. John Wesley was a failure-prone minister. And Billy Graham was dismissed from Bible college. These people were not used by God because they were spectacular; they were simply used spectacularly by God.

So where is the majority that God so eagerly calls and uses? It's the rest of us—you and me, who are the nobility of God's nobodies.

GOD'S CHOSEN NOBILITY

Are you old enough to remember the Miracle Mets? The original Mets baseball team was one of the greatest collections of lovable losers in history. The original 1962 Mets lost 120 games, but it wasn't the number they lost—it was the style they lost with! The manager was Casey Stengel, and the team was composed of castoffs from better teams—players like error-prone "Marvelous Marv" Throneberry. On his birthday, Stengel told him, "We was going to get you a birthday cake, but we figured you'd drop it." There was also Dick Stuart, known as "Dr. Strangeglove." By the end of the season, Stengel said, "This team has shown me ways of losing that I didn't even know existed."

Yet within seven years, the New York Mets had gone from the "Amazin' Mess" to the "Miracle Mets," when they beat the

Baltimore Orioles to become World Series champions. We all love this kind of story, the one about the underdog beating the odds. Hollywood tells it over and over in films such as *Rocky* or *The Mighty Ducks*. What excites us is the idea that nobody can be counted out, that success is possible for those willing to pay the price. If the New York Mets or Rocky Balboa can do it, we think, then maybe we could too.

The Bible, of course, tells the story of an underdog nation— Israel—that is the hope of the world because of God's special care for it. And it tells the story of the Savior of humanity coming from the least likely place at the least likely time to save us in the least likely way. He chose a group of followers who might have been the "Amazin' Mess" of their own day, as they constantly squabbled and nearly always missed the point. This is the great message of the Word of God: The issue is not our ability but God's. Therefore He is most glorified when the least likely hero wins out in His name.

Paul explained how it works in 1 Corinthians 1:27–28: "But God has chosen the foolish things of the world to put to shame the wise, and God has chosen the weak things of the world to put to shame the things which are mighty; and the base things of the world and the things which are despised God has chosen, and the things which are not, to bring to nothing the things that are." Did you catch the descriptions of God's heroes? *Foolish. Weak. Base. Despised.*

God can use the *foolish* of this world, those who are not well educated or intelligent. I think of D. L. Moody, a man with little education or polish. He had no degrees after his name, yet in addition to making him a great evangelist, God used him to establish Moody Press, Moody Bible Institute, and Moody radio stations. D. L. Moody serves as a good example that God's power for a passionate life is not dependent upon human intelligence, wisdom, or education.

God can use the *weak* of this world. Sometimes when we feel physically or spiritually worn out, we just want to take a long breather. Surely God can't use us when we're tired, we think. But look at Gideon in Judges 6. Gideon was hiding during a time of war when an angel of the Lord informed him that he would be the one to save Israel. Astonished, Gideon responded, "How can I save Israel? Indeed my clan is the weakest in Manasseh, and I am the least in my father's house" (v. 15).

Once God enlisted a nobody named Gideon, He gave him a nobody army—a mere three hundred soldiers to fight an army of thousands. But God took those nobodies and won a decisive battle. And He can use you, no matter how weak you may be. He can fill you with godly passion and use you to triumph over incredible odds.

God can also use the *base* of this world, the bottom of the barrel, those who most people would write off as worthless. Consider a few of the synonyms for base: low, dirty, sordid, contemptible, villainous, wretched, mean. This is about as far from noble as you can get. But God doesn't have a problem employing imperfect people in His service. Look at the kind of people He included in the genealogy of Jesus Christ: Tamar, who played the harlot; Ruth, a Gentile; Bathsheba, an adulteress; Rahab, a harlot. No matter what you have done in the past, God is willing and able to transform you and fill you with passion for life and service to Him.

WHY NOBODIES?

Why would God want to use the so-called nobodies in His kingdom? Wouldn't He be better served by enlisting the most gifted and talented, the strongest, and the most influential people? That question is answered in 1 Corinthians 1:29: God works with the simple, the weak, and the lowly so "that no flesh should glory in His presence." Or as Eugene Peterson paraphrased it in *The Message,* "That none of you can get by with blowing your own horn before God." Those who can accomplish great things on their own often want to take the credit for it. So God loves to use the lowly underdogs of His kingdom to accomplish great things, because they know they couldn't have done it without Him.

God knows that when we win against all probabilities, against insurmountable obstacles, and against overwhelming opposition despite any spectacular abilities or gifts of our own, then there can only be one conclusion: *God is powerful.* To God be the glory!

Bill Bright, founder of Campus Crusade for Christ, made a greater impact on the world than nearly anyone you could imagine. Through his organization and its evangelism, through the *Four Spiritual Laws* tract, through the *Jesus* film, and through an abundance of varied ministries, his influence for Christ penetrated virtually every nation on earth. Yet Dr. Bright was always quick to point out that he was surrounded by people more gifted in various ways than he was. He was not the grandest expositor of the Word or the most systematic theologian. He was simply a businessman who, along with his wife, Vonette, committed himself completely to Christ for more than fifty years. He was also a genuinely humble man, for he knew that God deserves all the glory and that God is pleased to work not through ability but through availability.

I hope you'll never again say the words "I can't," when talking about the work of God. You would be right, as long as you finish the phrase with, "but God can."

How Do You See Yourself?

In the world's eyes, you may be a nobody, but God knows the number of hairs on your head. He considers you important enough that He knows all there is to know about you, and He has His eye on you at every moment.

Sadly, we tend to listen to the world rather than to God. For example, if somebody calls you a real loser, you may begin to wonder if it's true, even though in God's eyes you are not a loser. Begin doubting yourself and the passion will flicker out. A life wide open will turn inward.

Where do we get these distorted pictures of ourselves? You brought into adulthood a view of yourself others foisted on you as a kid—more specifically, how your parents treated you. For example, if your mom or dad always called you "Gorgeous," you may have grown up seeing yourself as attractive. But if a parent nicknamed you "Dummy," it probably negatively colored your view of your intelligence. This influence also extends to other important adults in your life at that time, such as teachers, coaches, or ministers.

The culture in which you came of age also contributed to your self-view. All the early Barbie dolls were slender, blue-eyed blondes, representing the "ideal" girl. If you happened to be chubby with frizzy brown hair, you may have—with the unkind help of your peers—labeled yourself as second class. Sad to say, your church experience as a child or young person may have contributed to a negative self-view. If the church's emphasis was more on sin than on grace, you probably grew up viewing yourself as a "no-good sinner" instead of a "sinner saved by God's grace."

Now, as an adult, it's as if you carry a photograph of yourself everywhere you go—except the picture may be distorted by false information about the identity you naively accepted as a young person. So when your husband says, "You are beautiful," you compare that comment to your inner photo and say, "No, I'm not. I'm chubby and I have frizzy brown hair." Or if your wife says, "Honey, you're so wise," you quietly dismiss the comment, knowing that you're a dummy. And when God calls you to a life of passion, excitement, and adventure, you're pretty sure He's talking to the wrong person.

Have you considered the possibility that your lack of passion may spring from a lack of self-confidence? Think about the last time you found something you could really do well. Remember the passion you had for that activity? We give our heart, soul, and mind when we really believe we can make something happen. We need to believe that God will work powerfully through us. That's not conceit—it's faith in Him.

LIFE WIDE OPEN

The Real You

In his book *See Yourself As God Sees You,* Christian apologist Josh McDowell gives three foundational pillars to our true identity. Seeing yourself as God sees you will erode your self-doubt and fan the embers of your dying passion.

Pillar 1: You are lovable. God created you in His own image and loves you as His own child. God makes no mistakes. If He loves you—and He does—you are eternally lovable.

Pillar 2: You are valuable. God gave up His dear Son to reconcile you to Himself. If God gave such a ransom, you are indeed infinitely valuable.

Pillar 3: You are competent. You may not be the most talented, but God has gifted you and committed to you the supreme ministry of being His light in the world. If He is ready to trust you with a task of eternal proportions, you are thoroughly competent.[2]

Are you ready to turn from your self-doubt to accept what God says about you? As you do, He will ignite your passions and expand your dimension of greatness for Him, as described in this poem by an unknown author:

> No one can know the potential
> Of a life that is committed to win;
> With courage the challenge it faces,
> To achieve great success in the end!
>
> So explore the dimension of greatness
> And believe that the world can be won;
> Be a mind that is fully committed,
> Knowing the task can be done!
>
> Your world has no place for the skeptic,
> No room for the doubter to stand;

Me? No Way!

To weaken your firm resolution
That you can excel in this land!

We must have vision to see our potential,
And faith to believe what we see;
Then courage to act with conviction
To become what God meant us to be!

So possess the strength and the courage
To conquer whatever you choose;
It's the person who never gets started
That is destined forever to lose!

11

LIFE
UNLEASHING *the* POWER
WIDE
of a PASSIONATE LIFE
OPEN

Land of the Giants

F ROM THE TIME HE WAS FIVE, Hudson Taylor was consumed by an intense passion to be a missionary to China. He dedicated every thought and action toward that desire. He learned Mandarin Chinese, studied medicine, corresponded with mission agencies, spent his money in mission training, and above all else, waited for God to send him.

The young man prayed as if it all depended on God and worked as if it all depended on Hudson Taylor. He was convinced that he would never make it unless he learned to depend on God for everything. Toward that end, he put himself under strict daily training. He studied Latin, Greek, theology, and medicine while keeping up with his ordinary daily responsibilities. He flirted with the edges of financial disaster in order to allow God alone to meet his needs. He lived on a diet of oatmeal and rice and sent the savings to missionaries. Nobody would have questioned Hudson Taylor's passion.

He set sail for China in 1853, filled with hope and excitement. When he arrived, he found that those who were supposed to meet his ship had either died or fled. Rebels had overcome Shanghai. There was fighting in the streets, hostility toward westerners, and not a friend in sight. His support system had evaporated. So there stood a young Englishman, Hudson Taylor, staring at the face of a giant named China. I can't promise you that I wouldn't have climbed right back on the boat and booked homeward passage.

But then I'm not Hudson Taylor, who not only stayed in China but committed to going farther inland with the gospel. There had been missionaries around Shanghai, but no one had ever taken the Word of God to the vast, mysterious provinces of the hidden China. He faced illness, heartbreak, setbacks, hostility from the Chinese and from other missionaries, and—I'm certain—the occasional feeling of being overwhelmed. There were so many millions of unsaved people in China and so few missionaries. How could the lost souls ever be reached?

Taylor simply kept trusting God and facing down the giant. By the time he died, there was a significant and fruit-bearing Christian presence in inland China. Even the era of communism hasn't driven our faith out of that country. Hudson Taylor was the superior of that giant too.

When have you felt discouraged or overwhelmed? When have you felt that all your efforts were for naught, that maybe it was useless to go on trying? It's no fun to feel pint-sized when facing a giant. And that giant can take many forms. It could be one person or a group of people. It could be a problem. The giant could be financial in nature, or it may be something within yourself.

Anything that distracts us from our focus on Christ, detours us from our service for Him, and drains us of our driving passion is a giant that must be slain. In order to live life wide open in response to God's call, we must learn to take down the monsters that stand in the way of great accomplishment for God.

Who can show us how to be a giant-killer? My suggestion is that we couldn't do better than the shepherd boy named David. He was a kid who knew nothing about military strategy, yet he went one-on-one with a grizzled warrior—a card-carrying giant. Goliath stood nine feet tall and had the snarling attitude to match. He had paralyzed Israel's fighting force with his intimidating presence. He arrogantly mocked the children of Israel and their God. No one dared protest. With Goliath looming over them, this army—and the whole nation of Israel—was dead in the water.

GIANTS AT LARGE

Which giants have blocked your path to a life of passion? You may find some of them in this "rogues' gallery" of giant-sized problems to living wide open.

Resentment. Your spouse forgets to pick up the cleaning, and you sulk about it for hours. A church member sitting near you sings loudly and off key, and you can't resist scowling at him. A friend hasn't called you in several days, so you're not going to call her either. We all get slighted, ignored, offended, and hurt by other people. Resentment holds these offenses like a sponge instead of letting them roll off our back by living in grace and forgiveness.

Fear. Everybody is afraid of something. Israel was pinned down in fear of Goliath. What strikes terror in your heart? Flying? Spiders? The threat of nuclear war? The death of your spouse or child? A stock market collapse? To whatever extent you are immobilized by your fears, to that extent you will lack the full experience of passion in your life. Theologian Paul Tillich said, "Fear . . . has a definite object . . . which can be faced, analyzed, attacked, endured."[1] If you want to live wide open, the giant of fear may be your first enemy.

Discouragement. It is difficult to move forward through life at any speed when we have lost our courage or confidence. Things don't go the way we plan, so we get discouraged and give up. We fail at a task or a relationship, so we shrink back from entering into the next one. Discouragement tends to pull in the sails and toss out the anchor. "If it's going to be like this," we mutter, "why go on?" The giant of discouragement must be brought down.

Loneliness. God created us for intimate relationship with Himself and with others. We feel most alive and passionate when we are enjoying rich fellowship with the Lord, getting along well with family members, and having fun with friends. But we feel lost and cold when there is painful distance or division in our dearest relationships. The giant of loneliness scorns our attempts at living passionately.

Worry. British educator W. R. Inge once said, "Worry is interest paid on trouble before it falls due." Most people worry about things that will never happen. What a waste of emotional energy! Worry levies a burdensome tax on our joy and passion. It's difficult to charge into life wide open when you are worried about everything that could go wrong. No wonder Paul exhorted us, "Be anxious for nothing, but in everything by prayer and supplication, with thanksgiving, let your requests be made known to God" (Philippians 4:6).

Envy. Essayist Susan Sontag wrote, "I envy paranoids; they actually feel people are paying attention to them."[2] The envious person is fixated on the desire for what other people have—possessions, status, appearance, success, even passion for life. You are not free to enjoy the passionate life God has for you when the ogre of envy has you by the throat.

Guilt and shame. Psychologist and educator Lewis Smedes explained, "A person feels guilt because he did something wrong. A person feels shame because he is something wrong. . . . We may feel guilty because we lied to our mother. We may feel shame because we are not the person our mother wanted us to be."[3] Unresolved guilt and shame are deadly to a life of passion.

There are many more Goliaths in the army that lines up to challenge the passionate life. You may struggle against doubt, temptation, jealousy, procrastination, anger, rejection, bitterness, hopelessness, or another equally debilitating giant of a problem. You may be hindered from a life of passion by old scars and still-painful wounds inflicted by these brutes. If you hope to break through to the passion-filled life, you need to meet your Goliath head-on.

Most of us need our soul restored before we can become fully engaged in a life of passion. All the motivational pep talks and spiritual disciplines are hollow for the person who struggles with unresolved pain from the past and unconquered problems in the present. The path to passion for wounded people begins by choosing no longer to be your Goliath's victim and to take whatever steps God makes available to you to heal the past and help you move confidently into the future He has for you.

SLAYING YOUR GIANT

Do you feel small compared to your present-day Goliath? Perhaps you feel too weak or inadequate to put up a fight. Giants can be intimidating, as King Saul and the army of Israel knew. But God has empowered us and equipped us to bring them down. Let's take several points of instruction from David's triumph over Goliath, as recorded in 1 Samuel 17.

1. *Confront your giant.* When Goliath, the jumbo-sized Philistine, taunted Israel and dared them to send someone to fight him, Saul and all the Israelites "were dismayed and greatly afraid" (v. 11). King Saul had a history of being a mighty warrior. He should have picked up the gauntlet and confronted Goliath in the power of the Lord. Yet Saul, along with the whole army, stood there quaking in his sandals. Do you think God could have used Saul to slay the giant? Absolutely! But since the warrior-king was too fearful to confront Goliath, God had to look for someone else.

The first step in getting past your problem to a passionate life is to confront your giant head-on. Here's a good place to start: Turn to a fresh journal page and identify in writing the giants you are facing. Write down their names: guilt, envy, fear—whatever they are. Describe them. For example, you may write something like, "I feel guilty for what I've done in the past" or, "I harbor resentment toward my spouse for his/her insensitivity toward me" or, "If I give myself fully to God, I'm afraid He might ask me to do something I don't want to do." Add specific examples of how your giant has terrorized you. The more you get down on paper, the clearer your Goliath will be in your sight.

2. *Remain consistent in preparation.* David the shepherd boy may have been young, small, and inexperienced in military combat; but he was not unprepared for meeting Goliath. For one thing, the boldness and naiveté of youth was on his side. Remember some of the daredevil things we did as kids, when we didn't know enough to be scared? Those were the days when it seemed easier to ask forgiveness after the fact than to ask permission ahead of time. As Pearl S. Buck has said, "The young do not know enough to be prudent, and therefore they attempt the impossible, and achieve it, generation after generation." That's probably where David was.

Long before his dramatic showdown with Goliath in the Valley of Elah, David had defended sheep on the hillsides of Bethlehem. He explained to Saul that watching sheep had involved facing the occasional lion or bear; when some predator attacked the sheep, he simply killed it (see vv. 34–35). David had learned courage when nobody was around to see it. It was his consistent integrity and commitment that prepared him to meet Goliath when that moment came.

As a giant-slayer, you prepare for battle by practicing consistency in your spiritual disciplines. You must spend time faithfully and privately before God, poring over His instruction manual for spiritual battle—the Word of God. You must humble yourself in prayer before your "Commander in Chief," just as Joshua did prior to the battle of Jericho (see Joshua 5:13–15). Don't skip any of these routine steps hoping to jump ahead of God's schedule. God desires to train you in private through consistent personal discipline.

3. *Consider the cost.* Author Ray Bradbury said, "Living at risk is jumping off the cliff and building your wings on the way down." Taking on a menacing giant involves some risk. After all, this is war. In fighting for what is rightfully yours, you will still be under enemy fire. People have wondered why David carried five stones in his pouch when he needed only one to fell Goliath. Perhaps he

would not presume that his first shot would do the trick. He probably expected some kind of battle, slinging stones, dodging Goliath's big javelin. He was confident about victory, but he may have approached Goliath wondering if he would be wounded in the skirmish. At some point the shepherd boy considered the cost and took the risk.

If you want to achieve great things in your life, you'd better be ready for risk-taking. Theodore Roosevelt said, "Far better is it to dare mighty things, to win glorious triumphs, even though checkered with failure, than to take rank with those poor spirits who neither enjoy much nor suffer much, because they live in the gray twilight that knows not victory nor defeat." If you're a Christian, you know that the "gray twilight" he's talking about isn't mysterious or elusive. It's called lack of faith. We can risk the cost of battle because Jesus promised, "All things are possible to him who believes" (Mark 9:23).

When you go to war against your giants, it probably won't be easy, and you likely won't dispense your problem with one shot. You may be in for a long battle. It may get worse before it gets better. You may take a hit or two along the way. But if the skirmish gets you past this giant and on the road to the passionate life you desire, it's worth the risk. Consider these lines from an anonymous author:

To laugh is to risk appearing the fool.
To weep is to risk appearing sentimental.
To reach for another is to risk involvement.
To expose your ideas, your dreams, before a crowd is to risk their
    loss.
To love is to risk not being loved in return.
To live is to risk dying.
To believe is to risk failure.
But risks must be taken,
because the greatest hazard to life is to risk nothing.

121

The people who risk nothing, have nothing, are nothing.

They may avoid suffering and sorrow,

but they cannot learn, feel, change, grow, love, live.

Chained by their attitudes, they are slaves;

they have forfeited their freedom.

Only a person who risks is free.

4. *Be courageous in battle.* King Saul attempted to equip David for battle by outfitting him in his own battle armor. You need to remember that Saul was a big man, at least a head taller than his peers (see 1 Samuel 9:2), but David was just a kid. After trying to walk in the armor, David declined the offer. He didn't need armor and a big sword when defending his sheep. His strength and protection were in the power of the Spirit. David announced, "The LORD, who delivered me from the paw of the lion and from the paw of the bear, He will deliver me from the hand of this Philistine" (1 Samuel 17:37). So he courageously marched out to battle with five small stones and one big God.

There have been times in your life when you have seen God knock your big problems down to size. Reflect upon those victories. Replay them in your heart and mind. Take courage and "be strong in the Lord and in the power of His might" (Ephesians 6:10). As someone has said, you plus God equals a majority. No giant can withstand you when you are led and empowered by God's Spirit.

5. *Be a champion for God.* When you step out boldly to confront your giant, you join the ranks of God's army of champions. David is in that brave band, as is Moses, Joshua, Gideon, Samson, Peter, Paul, and countless numbers of heroic warriors in the pages of the Bible.

But be aware that when you move out as God's champion, you may be criticized by others, even by those closest to you. Some family members and friends may feel threatened as you step out in the Spirit to pursue your passion. When David showed up on the front lines and began inquiring about Goliath, his own family shot him down. His eldest brother said, "Why did you come down here? And with whom have you left those few sheep in the wilderness? I know your pride and the insolence of your heart, for you have come down to see the battle" (1 Samuel 17:28). Instead of lauding David's courage, his brothers chided him for abandoning the sheep.

Like David, silence your critics with your courage, determination, and trust in God. The Spirit-empowered shepherd boy strode confidently into battle armed with a sling and five stones. The first stone flew and found its mark. Goliath toppled like a felled tree, and Israel enjoyed a great victory and new freedom to be God's people in the world.

The same God who brought victory to an underdog shepherd boy stands ready to help you conquer your giants and to free you to the passionate life He created you to enjoy. Like David, you have a choice before you: You can remain paralyzed by your pain or problems, going nowhere; or you can face them, overcome them, and follow your passions.

6. *Don't give in to the giant of false humility.* There are a few confused saints among us who have taken that notion that Christians should not desire success. Imagine David saying, "Oh, but God wants me to be humble, and I'd look so pompous challenging giants." I suggest you read these words from Erwin Raphael McManus and take them to heart:

> It is important to note that ambition is not wrong. In fact, the Bible never speaks of ambition itself as negative. Ambition is a God-given motivation. One of the great tragedies among many followers of Christ is the loss of ambition after coming to faith. They have become convinced that any personal ambition is dishonoring to God. I have met some who have gone as far as to only do the opposite of what they desired because they were so persuaded that any passion to achieve had to be rejected and overcome. The simple reasoning is "it can't be God's will if I want to do it."[4]

If you want to do it, and it's something you know God wants done, then ambition is just another gift God has given you for the task. Ambition can be a very important element of your passion. So move forward and don't be so critical of yourself. Move forward to the glory of God, and you'll begin to see the giants fall.

12

LIFE
UNLEASHING *the* POWER
WIDE
of a PASSIONATE LIFE
OPEN

Soar above Your Circumstances

IN DECEMBER 1914, British explorer Sir Ernest Shackleton led a crew of twenty-eight on an exciting mission to uncharted territory. The team departed from South Georgia Island in the Falkland Islands and sailed for Antarctica. Their ship was called the *Endurance,* and rarely has there been a more prophetic name for a sea vessel.

While still one hundred miles from the coast of Antarctica, the *Endurance* locked up in the surface ice. The frozen sea halted the voyage and placed the crew in grave danger. For nine months the frozen ocean slowly dragged the ship away from the continent. Can you imagine how it must have felt to be part of that crew? Finally the ice crushed and sank the vessel in November 1915.

The crew survived, however, and set out on the long journey home. They walked four hundred miles across the ice, towing the *Endurance*'s three lifeboats and anything they could salvage from her. Traversing ice and water, they made it to barren, frozen Elephant Island, setting foot on soil for the first time in 497 days. But they were still hundreds of miles from their point of embarkation.

Shackleton and five others set out for South Georgia Island in one of the lifeboats. They courageously traveled eight hundred miles across the fiercest waters on the planet, the South Atlantic Ocean.

Seventeen days after leaving Elephant Island, and almost a year and a half after launching the expedition, the lifeboat arrived at South Georgia Island. Shackleton and the others returned to Elephant Island in a Chilean vessel to rescue the remainder of the crew. Miraculously, not one crew member was lost in the ordeal. Think about the environmental conditions, the lack of necessities, and perhaps above all the crushing demoralization they endured—yet they stood the test.

These men wore the same clothes, frozen stiff on their bodies, for months. Many of them suffered frostbite in the unrelenting, subzero temperatures. Their diet consisted largely of penguin and eventually their own sled dogs. Yet they persisted. Why?

It seems clear that the key was Shackleton himself. He was a man of purpose and passion. The boat may have gone down, but his spirit was unsinkable. He kept the crew focused on survival, and he got every one of them home to Britain.

If you had been a member of Shackleton's crew, how would you have responded to the grueling eighteen-month ordeal? Would you have persisted and persevered? Or would you have been tempted to give up and die?

We are not meant to trudge sadly along as victims of our problems. God has equipped us with wings to soar above them. The prophet Isaiah, inspired by the Holy Spirit, wrote some of the most majestic words of all time in describing the indomitable human spirit that prevails in the strength of God:

> He gives power to the weak,
> And to those who have no might He increases strength.
> Even the youths shall faint and be weary,
> And the young men shall utterly fall,
> But those who wait on the LORD
> Shall renew their strength;
> They shall mount up with wings like eagles,
> They shall run and not be weary,
> They shall walk and not faint. (Isaiah 40:29–31)

Certainly you've had your passion dampened by defeat and discouragement. More than once you've spread your wings, only to be shot down in flames. Welcome to the club—we call it the human race. In our club, nobody succeeds every single time. As a matter of fact, we like to talk about the fact that the very best hitters in baseball fail to reach base two out of three times at bat. We remind each other with a smile that the greatest inventions and discoveries of humanity have come to people who failed more than their share of times.

But you argue that there are setbacks, and then there are *setbacks*. You're right, of course. Sometimes we're blindsided by something life-shattering. Sometimes there are bad days, but sometimes there are true crises when the ship hits the ice and sinks like a stone. We can't minimize the experience of a catastrophe. What we can do is recognize that the way we face the unexpected will make a significant difference in how we come through the storm.

You can respond like Job's wife, whose counsel to her stricken husband was, "Do you still hold fast to your integrity? Curse God and die!" (Job 2:9). Or you can hold fast to your integrity—as Ernest Shackleton did; as Job did, stripped of his family, his possessions, and his health; as Joseph did, sitting in the darkness of an Egyptian prison; and, in the ultimate sense, as Jesus did, cursed and rejected, mocked and taunted, stripped and crucified. In all these occasions, the crisis became a moment of shining triumph in the end because the afflicted held fast to his integrity. And in those moments, the angels rejoice in every hallway of heaven.

Bill Russell, legendary center for the Boston Celtics basketball team, used to keep his own personal scorecard. He graded himself after every game on a scale of one to one hundred. In his career, he never achieved more than sixty-five. Given the way most of us are taught to think about goals, we would regard Russell as an abject failure. The poor soul played in twelve hundred ball games and never achieved his standard. Yet it was striving for that standard that made him one of the greatest men ever to play the game.[1]

127

LIFE WIDE OPEN

An employee in a large corporation made a mistake that cost the company a million dollars. The man was called in to see the boss, and he fully expected to be fired. But his boss had a different approach.

"Do you know the secret of making a million dollars?" asked the boss. "It's making good decisions. And do you know the secret of making good decisions? It's making bad decisions and learning from them. I've just invested a million dollars in you, so learn from your mistake. It may turn out to be a reasonably priced lesson after all."

Passionate people learn from their failures. Failure is one of life's greatest teachers—or it certainly can be if we choose to learn from it rather than let it crush us. What are some of the lessons learners gain from their failures? Here are just a few:

- Failure teaches us to depend on God.
- Failure teaches us humility.
- Failure teaches us that we can't always get what we want.
- Failure teaches us to make a correction in our course of action.
- Failure teaches us character.
- Failure teaches us perseverance.
- Failure teaches us that we can endure and survive.

In terms of personal failure and defeat, I like to divide people into two categories: learners and nonlearners. When learners make a mistake or fail at a task, they are less likely to repeat it. Nonlearners are destined to fail again and again. When learners do something that works, they will probably do it even better the next time. Nonlearners are hard-pressed even to repeat the victory.

George Eliot once said, "It's never too late to become the person you could have been." I would go on to say that you are destined to remain the person you have always been, lacking the passion and joy in life you desire, unless you learn from your failures and defeats.

KEEP COMING BACK FOR MORE

Passionate people hang in there when the going gets tough. They persist, they persevere, they never lose heart, and they never quit. Proverbs 24:16 says, "For a righteous man may fall seven times and rise again." Jesus told the parable of the persistent widow "that men always ought to pray and not lose heart" (Luke 18:1). Combine these two scriptural principles, and you have the idea of a person who keeps praying and keeps persisting until success is certain—an unbeatable formula.

The apostle Paul urged that we be "not lagging in diligence, fervent in spirit, serving the Lord" (Romans 12:11). And he said to the Corinthian Christians, "But we have this treasure in earthen vessels, that the excellence of the power may be of God and not of us. . . . Therefore we do not lose heart. Even though our outward man is perishing, yet the inward man is being renewed day by day" (2 Corinthians 4:7, 16).

That "inward man," of course, is the key. When the torrential storm came and the outside world was in turmoil, what kept Job or Joseph or Jesus moving forward was the calm at the eye of the storm—the powerful faith that even if every worldly possession was washed away, even if the earth opened up beneath them, God was unmovable and steadfast. And the best part is that this "inward man"—that spiritual passion—is renewed every single day. Here is the powerful inner strength that endures when the hurricane descends upon us:

> God is our refuge and strength,
> A very present help in trouble.
> Therefore we will not fear,

Even though the earth be removed,
And though the mountains be carried into the midst of the sea;
Though its waters roar and be troubled,
Though the mountains shake with its swelling. (Psalm 46:1–3)

If you have that truth locked in your heart, you will keep coming back for more. You will have the passion of Peter, the Rock. During his three years on earth with Jesus, Peter humiliated himself more than once. But the important thing in the end was not his failure but his resilience. Peter was the disciple who walked on water toward Jesus until his faith gave out and he started to sink (see Matthew 14:22–32). Was it more important that he failed or that he got far enough to learn the lesson of faith?

Later, Jesus quizzed the disciples on His true identity. Peter blurted out, "You are the Christ, the Son of the living God" (Matthew 16:16). Jesus blessed him for his answer. But only moments later, as Jesus foretold His coming death, Peter took it upon himself to reprove the Master: "Far be it from You, Lord; this shall not happen to You!" (v. 22). Instead of a blessing from the Lord, Peter received a scathing rebuke: "Get behind Me, Satan! You are an offense to Me" (v. 23).

How would you feel if you were called on the carpet by your church's leadership and accused of being an instrument of the devil—and the rebuke was justified? Would you be tempted to crawl into a hole and never come out? Start shopping for a new church? Yet was it more important for Peter that he misspoke or that he learned the lesson of obedience?

Peter blew it again big time in the final hours of Christ's life on earth. When Jesus announced in the Upper Room that His disciples would stumble, Peter insisted, "Even if all are made to stumble because of You, I will never be made to stumble. . . . Even if I have to die with You, I will not deny You!" (Matthew 26:33, 35). But he did, only hours later denying three times that he even knew the Master. One of the most anguished scenes in the Gospels is that of our Lord gazing at Peter as the rooster crowed. Peter was destroyed with shame and grief, and he went outside and wept bitterly (see Luke 22:60–62).

But that wasn't the end of Peter. Ashamed, disillusioned, discouraged? Yes. Bail out, run away, quit? Never! When Peter heard that Jesus had risen, he sprinted to the tomb and marveled at what had happened (see Luke 24:12). When he saw the risen Christ on the shore while he was fishing, Peter plunged into the sea, apparently excited to see Him (see John 21:7). When Jesus gently questioned him, Peter affirmed his love for the Master. Peter was among those in the Upper Room filled with the Holy Spirit on the Day of Pentecost. And the early chapters of the book of Acts record the astounding, Spirit-empowered exploits of an imperfect disciple who would not give in to his foibles and failures.

In an earlier chapter we talked about William Carey, the cobbler who became the father of modern missions. Carey had a world of obstacles to face. As a child, he was sickly, afflicted by numerous allergies. He was also poorly educated and prone to failure. He tried teaching school and failed. He tried pastoring and failed yet again. But once his burden for the lost world ignited his passion, he was unstoppable.

When Carey announced that he would leave England for India, his fellow ministers thought he had lost his mind. His wife and parents also thought he had taken leave of his senses, but he wouldn't let go of his vision. When the authorities in India didn't want him, when his fellow missionary was caught in dishonest schemes, when there were no converts, and even when his printing press burned down, William Carey would not give up.

Once he reached his mission field, Carey didn't take a furlough or return to England in forty-one years. In addition to translating the Bible, he founded more than one hundred rural schools for the people of India. He founded Serampore College, which is still training ministers today. He introduced the concept of a savings bank to the farmers of India. He published the first Indian newspaper. He wrote dictionaries and grammars in five different languages. He so influenced the nation of India that, largely through his efforts, the practice of sati—the burning of widows—was outlawed.

What was William Carey's secret? His brother, Thomas, once said about him, "I . . . recollect that he was, from a boy . . . always resolutely determined never to give up at any point or particle of anything on which his mind was set."

The following poem, by an unknown author, could have just as easily been penned by William Carey, by the apostle Peter, by Job or Joseph, by Jesus or by countless followers of Jesus. It is entitled simply, "Don't Quit":

> When things go wrong as they sometimes will,
> When the road you're trudging seems all uphill.
> When the funds are low and the debts are high,
> And you want to smile but you have to sigh.
> When care is pressing you down a bit—
> Rest if you must, but don't you quit.
>
> Success is failure turned inside out,
> The silver tint of the clouds of doubt.
> And you never can tell how close you are,
> It may be near when it seems afar.
> So stick to the fight when you're hardest hit—
> It's when things go wrong that you mustn't quit.

LOOKING FORWARD TO OUR TRUE HOME

There's another reason that keeps passionate people fighting to the end, which can be illustrated by Sir Ernest Shackleton and his crew. Shackleton inspired his men to keep pressing on because they were going home. They had left family and friends in England and Ireland, the lands of their citizenship. Giving up meant never seeing their loved ones again. They kept struggling onward because journey's end was well worth the effort.

That's why, today, you and I struggle forward. That's why you will rise again tomorrow to take up the tools in your hand, the strength in your shoulders, and the firm resolution in your heart, and you will keep chipping away at the great goal God has given you. That's why the passion inside you, the inward man, is renewed every day—because of *home*. And it's not the home where you will lay your head tonight, but your *true* home. It is the home where you and I will finally see the Master face to face.

The home here on earth is like the crude shack on Elephant Island where Shackleton's crew huddled together for warmth, living off the meager scraps of food available to them. As they ate those few sour bites, they could still think of the feast that awaited them in England upon their return. And in that imagining, in the foretaste of glory, they could push through one more day.

It's like that for you and me. Scripture tells us, "Our citizenship is in heaven" (Philippians 3:20). We're only strangers and pilgrims here, passing through on our way to a glorious Promised Land. The road is long and filled with obstacles, but we claim this passage from Hebrews as our rallying cry:

> These all died in faith, not having received the promises, but having seen them afar off were assured of them, embraced them and confessed that they were strangers and pilgrims on the earth. For those who say such things declare plainly that they seek a homeland. And truly if they had called to mind that country from which they had come out, they would have had opportunity to return. But now they desire a better, that is, a heavenly country. Therefore God is not ashamed to be called their God, for He has prepared a city for them. (Hebrews 11:13–16)

"Opportunity to return," you say? That's not much of an opportunity at all. Yes, we could turn back. We could renounce our passion and the life wide open on the road to glory—but what would we be returning to? Little but the dust of death. And what awaits us instead? "A heavenly country . . . [where] God is not ashamed to be called our God, for He has prepared a city for us."

I don't know about you, but just reading those words renews my inward man. It stokes my passion until the flames leap upward inside me. It gives me strength not only for surviving but for thriving—even if those crises be mortal ones. We know now that God is not only the destination but a member of the traveling party. He has promised to be with us always.

And so we'll keep walking, keep soldiering on—and at some point, in the words of Isaiah, we'll mount up with wings as eagles and soar across those final miles to the land where we will finally run and not be weary; we will walk and never faint.

Part III

LIFE
UNLEASHING *the* POWER
WIDE
of a PASSIONATE LIFE
OPEN

Unleash the Power of the Passionate Life

THE OLD PROSPECTOR leaned close to the campfire so the light of the flames would illuminate the yellowed, stained map in his hands. He pored carefully over the faint markings, as he'd done every day of his quest. A treasure beyond his wildest dreams was hidden somewhere in the cave. It was his for the taking because he alone possessed the old map. Without the tattered chart before him, the prospector had little prospect in life. But if he followed the map to the detail, more treasure than he could never earn in a hundred lifetimes would be his.

Deeper into the cave pressed the old prospector. He turned where the map directed him to turn. He climbed where the map said to climb. Then he dug by torchlight at the very spot indicated on the map by a large X. Deeper and deeper until—*chunk!*—the small spade struck wood. The old man's heart raced wildly as he unearthed the old chest and lifted the lid. And there it was—the treasure that would forever change his life!

You and I have embarked on a treasure hunt far more exciting. The life of fulfillment we seek is the key to eternal life, to unbroken joy, to every pure and happy thing imaginable. No way can we manufacture or earn through our own efforts all He has for us. But we need one thing—*the map!*

God has not buried this treasure in a remote cave as if to hide it from us. But neither does He simply pour His riches into our hands. He knows that the real adventure is in the quest; He knows that the most joy comes in the pursuit. God's Word is our treasure map, and His Spirit is our guide into the uncharted lands we must explore. In these concluding chapters, we'll discover the biblical guidelines for the life of passion and adventure.

LIFE
UNLEASHING the POWER
WIDE
of a PASSIONATE LIFE
OPEN

Remember What It's All About

BECAUSE SOCIETIES HAVE A NEED TO REMEMBER, we fill our
world with monuments. The Statue of Liberty reminds us about
the beauty and grace of freedom. The Tomb of the Unknown
Soldier helps us never to forget the countless numbers of soldiers
who gave their life for that freedom. Take a walk through your city
or town and I imagine you'll find monuments and historical
plaques placed by your chamber of commerce.

Naturally, we like monuments that inspire us—the general on
his stallion, sword in the air, his horse rearing backward; the
pioneer's open hand raised to the heavens. Our statues commemorate larger-than-life heroes—or, in one case, a smaller-than-small
insect. Enterprise, Alabama, has on its main street a tall statue of a
boll weevil. Of all creatures, an insect; and of all insects, a particularly destructive one. Why would the town want to commemorate
a six-legged parasite? The answer is that those who erected the
statue were not celebrating the insect but the God whom they
believe used the small beetle.

Like much of the South, this part of Alabama was once cotton
country. The region was totally dependent upon King Cotton. But
then in 1915 came a pestilence from the direction of Mexico—the
little insect that averages one-quarter of an inch in length but can

destroy thousands of acres of cotton by puncturing the boll, or pod, of the cotton to lay its eggs. In no time, the region lost its ability to bring its crop to maturity. Enterprise was looking economic disaster in the face.

But necessity is the mother of invention, and a number of scientists including George Washington Carver were roused to investigate alternative crops. The peanut, it was discovered, could be planted and harvested very efficiently. Farmers diversified in many other directions, and the economy was better off than ever before.

Many people saw the hand of God in this trial. They felt that God had used the little boll weevil to guide them toward the demands of a modern economy. And in 1919 the monument was placed in the town's central location so that the people might never forget—a towering statue of a woman holding a large boll weevil over her head.

Monuments are important not only to us but to God. Without the lessons of history, we are helpless to face the challenges of the future. Throughout the Bible, God led His people to memorialize the great moments. Here are some of the highlights of biblical monuments:

- *Offerings and sacrifices,* which were tangible reminders of an element of God's relationship with the people of Israel.

- *Blue tassels,* placed on the corners of the people's garments at the Lord's command that they might "remember all the commandments of the LORD and do them" (Numbers 15:39).

- *National festivals,* such as Passover. These celebrations reenacted God's miraculous activity in Israel's history (see Exodus 12:26–27).

- *A riverside monument* upon crossing the Jordan into Canaan, built from stones pulled from the dry riverbed. It was to help people remember how God dried up the river, facilitating the invasion (see Joshua 4:4–7).

Perhaps the most significant memorial of all was instituted by Jesus in the Upper Room the night before He was crucified. Jesus served His disciples bread and wine, representing His broken body and shed blood, commanding them to partake "in remembrance of Me" (Luke 22:19). The apostle Paul instructed the church to continue this practice to "proclaim the Lord's death until He comes" (1 Corinthians 11:26). Communion in worship, the Lord's Supper, is a living memorial to pass the Upper Room experience from generation to generation.

God knows that our life is "but vapor that appears for a little time and then vanishes away" (James 4:14). If our life is a vapor, our memories are misty at best. Our Lord works patiently to remind us, because in the wealth of experience comes the wealth of wisdom. When we forget, we are like children prone to every poor decision imaginable.

That kind of stumbling, fumbling life without memory drains us of all passion. To put the pedal to the metal in the life wide open, we need good rearview mirrors—and to remember, as those mirrors tell us, that "reflected objects are larger than they appear."

What must we remember for maximizing our passion?

IT'S ALL ABOUT GOD

We need to continually remember what the passionate life is all about and who it's for. Let me get right to the point: It's not *about* you, and it's not *for* you.

Don't get me wrong: The passionate life God desires to lead you into will be the most fulfilling and satisfying life you could ever imagine. It's not an easy, pain-free, trouble-free life, but it brings a great sense of accomplishment. Yet God doesn't call you to a passionate life for your enjoyment and satisfaction. It's all about Him, bringing glory to God and sharing His life with others. Here are a few specific things to remember.

1. *Remember who—and whose—you are.* Every spoke in the

wheel of your life goes back to the center, which is God. Being His child is the all-determining factor in your life. It defines what kind of person you are, what kind of motives you have, what kind of values you hold dear, and what kind of husband, wife, son, daughter, friend, employee, or boss you are. *You are not your own;* you belong to Christ. He has bought you with the ultimate price. When you said yes to Him, you were freed from the despair of sin so that He might become your master in every aspect of your existence. He is the only master who will bring you joy and blessing rather than consuming and destroying you.

Even having declared Him as Lord, even being transformed by His Spirit, you will experience "spiritual entropy." That is, you will gravitate back toward disorder, chaos, self-rule, and self-destruction. Time after time He will bring you joy in some area—say, your marriage—and you will slowly try to reseize the throne. This tension between God's rule and your rule will strip you of all passion, because you cannot serve two masters. You must choose, and only one possible choice will lead you back to the passionate, full-speed-ahead life.

God loves you so deeply, so perfectly. He knows what will bring you joy and what will surely lead you to despair. His passion is for you to come to passion, as Saint Augustine expressed in these remarkable words from his *Confessions:*

> You called, you cried, you shattered my deafness.
> You sparkled, you blazed, you drove away my blindness.
> You shed your fragrance, and I drew in my breath, and I pant for you.
> I tasted and I now hunger and thirst.
> You touched me, and I now burn with longing for your peace.[1]

2. *Remember your purpose.* Life wide open is centered in the Great Commandment (see Matthew 22:37–39); it's all about loving God and loving people. If you were to place these two central missions in the center of a piece of paper, you could make a

diagram, working outward, of how they translate to your work, your family, your church involvement, and everything else. Keeping God and people at the top of your priorities at every moment would totally revolutionize your life—every vestige of self-centeredness would drain out as you found the joy of being connected to your Lord and your cotravelers through life. The life wide open is the very antithesis of the self-absorbed life. And self-absorption, I'm sure you've discovered, is the very opposite of joy.

3. *Remember to live in the presence of God.* At the very core of a life of passion is living continually in the presence of God. That's the essence of true worship. Life wide open is a life of awe and wonder at the God we love and serve. Living such a life requires a single focus on one thing and one thing only. A writer from another generation captured this in this statement:

> A zealous man in religion is preeminently a man of one thing . . . he sees only one thing, he cares for one thing, he lives for one thing, he is swallowed up for one thing; and that one thing is to please God. Whether he lives, or whether he dies, whether he has health, or whether he has sickness, whether he is rich, or whether he is poor, whether he pleases man, or whether he gives offense, whether he is thought wise, or whether he is thought foolish, whether he gets honor, or whether he gets shame, for all this . . . the man cares nothing at all. He burns for one thing; and that one thing is to please God and to advance God's glory.[2]

Here is the goal of your every day: seeing every corner of your world infiltrated by the incredible presence of God, until every ounce of darkness is driven away.

> God be in my head,
> and in my understanding.
> God be in mine eyes
> and in my looking.

God be in my mouth
and in my speaking.
God be in my heart
and in my thinking.
God be at my end
and at my departing.[3]

It's All about Surrender

You said yes to Christ on the day He entered your life—and you felt a new passion, a new appetite for living, a new joy, and a new peace. But unless that occurred recently, you have made another discovery: You have to continue saying yes, every single day.

In other words, the great war for your soul was won on that day when Christ came into your heart. But the skirmishes continue. Being a human being with imperfect human desires, you keep straggling away from the Victor's camp, with its joyful celebration, and slipping back into the dark lair of the enemy. You could find sanctuary and security forever within the walls of God's protection, but something within you is prone to wander. You are like the Japanese soldiers who were discovered in South Pacific caves long after World War II was over—still living in fear and eating insects and roots even though the war was over and home awaited them.

Part of our passion comes from the daily realization that *we are winners*. To the victor go the spoils, and we enjoy every benefit of the victory that was won on Calvary, when Christ defeated death. Now we need only surrender fully to Him and serve under His command. When we realize that our future is secured, that there is no way Satan can snatch us from God's hand, we take on the positive and exuberant spirit of champions.

But how exactly do we surrender? As we share in Christ's victory, we share in His crucifixion. As we become Christians, we are crucified with Him (see Romans 6:6; Galatians 2:20). That means all the self-defeating parts of us—the rebelliousness, the strife, the resentment, the selfishness, the slavery to our lusts—all these things are nailed to the cross with Christ. It is the sum of those evils, what we call the *old self,* that is crucified. Then as surely as Christ rose in perfect form on the third day, we rise again to walk in newness of life, in passion, and in the spirit of champions.

If only we could remember! If only we could surround ourselves with monuments and memorials—the Statue of True Liberty; the Tomb of the Unknown Sinner—to keep ourselves from forgetting, even for an instant, that we need no longer struggle with a defeated enemy. This is why we must build into our life the systems and monuments for remembering.

Do you remember the ending of the movie *It's a Wonderful Life?* In that great film, George Bailey, played by Jimmy Stewart, is joyful—uncontrollably joyful, laughing-hysterically joyful. Why? Because he has been allowed by heaven to see the way things really are. I won't suggest that the theology of angels is biblical in that movie, but the point is solid: God is using us in ways we cannot expect, just like He used a boll weevil and just like He has used trials and frustrations in your life. He is painting a picture you won't see and appreciate until some later day when you can step back and take in the whole canvas. If an angel came down to earth today and allowed you to see the spiritual reality of your life—the fact that the battle is won and that absolutely nothing stands between you and the joyful life God wants you to have, you would respond just like George Bailey. At the end of that movie he kisses his wife with passion; he embraces his children with passion; he completely embodies the passion of a life that has been thrown wide open by seeing things the way they were all along, if only he'd had God's perspective.

That's why we surrender daily. We know something in us forgets and tries to wander back out into the darkness—back out into defeat. We want to live in victory like the champions God has made us. So daily we come before God, affirm that those sinful parts of us have been nailed to the cross, and make ourselves living sacrifices once again. The ultimate sacrifice was made at Calvary, but there is also daily sacrifice on our part because our memory is so poor.

Who are our models of the passionate life energized by total surrender?

1. *Job.* We have looked at him briefly in another chapter. This man was assailed by greater calamities in two days than most of us will ever face in a lifetime. In a test to demonstrate his integrity, Job was deprived of his family, his wealth, and his good health—in only two days! Yet Job responded with utter surrender: "He fell to the ground and worshiped. . . . 'The LORD gave, and the LORD has taken away; blessed be the name of the LORD.' In all this Job did not sin nor charge God with wrong" (Job 1:20–22).

How do we respond in our tests and trials, which are miniscule compared to Job's grief? The car breaks down, a friend dies from cancer, a job layoff strains the bank account—and in our pride we want to rise up and fight God about what's happening to us. Now, surrender does not imply that we should be less than responsible and resourceful in dealing with difficult life situations. Rather, it means doing whatever God gives you to do and praising Him for the results, even if they are painful or unpleasant.

2. *Jonah.* He surrendered and worked passionately for God—after being dragged, kicking and screaming, to the point of obedience. God commanded him, "Arise, go to Nineveh, that great city, and cry out against it; for their wickedness has come up before Me" (Jonah 1:2). Jonah didn't happen to like that particular group of Gentiles, so he ran the other way. He booked passage on a ship headed in the opposite direction. You know the rest of the story: Jonah was tossed overboard during a violent storm and gobbled up by a great fish.

It didn't take Jonah long in the belly of the fish to realize that his independence had made his life worse, not better. Perhaps you have made a similar discovery—or need to. You might want to borrow Jonah's prayer of surrender: "I will sacrifice to You with the voice of thanksgiving; I will pay what I have vowed. Salvation is of the

Lord" (Jonah 2:9). In New Testament language he might have said, "I have been crucified with Christ; now I intend to live out my surrender."

Even though he went on to Nineveh and spearheaded a spiritual revival as commanded, Jonah still battled a spirit of independence (see Jonah 4). A moment-by-moment life of passion in Christ requires moment-by-moment surrender to Christ.

3. *Zacchaeus.* Kids love this short story about a short man, providing a tall lesson about sincere surrender to Christ. Jesus engaged the curious Zacchaeus as he sat in a sycamore tree, and the man surrendered his life to the Master (see Luke 19:2–10). But notice how Zacchaeus's statement of surrender included his behavior, not just his belief: "Look, Lord, I give half of my goods to the poor; and if I have taken anything from anyone by false accusation, I restore fourfold" (v. 8). Passionate people have a way of acting extravagantly, letting their joy bubble out into their actions.

4. *Paul.* When it comes to surrender, the apostle Paul had no peer. He signed over everything to the Master—his mission in life, his possessions, his safety, his schedule, and his very life. His surrender is clearly summarized in Philippians 3:8: "Yet indeed I also count all things loss for the excellence of the knowledge of Christ Jesus my Lord, for whom I have suffered the loss of all things, and count them as rubbish, that I may gain Christ."

Eugene Peterson's paraphrase makes Paul's surrender even more graphic: "All the things I once thought were so important are gone from my life. Compared to the high privilege of knowing Christ Jesus as my Master, firsthand, everything I once thought I had going for me is insignificant. . . . I've dumped it all in the trash so that I could embrace Christ and be embraced by Him" (v. 8 MSG).

Launching into life wide open by surrendering fully to Christ doesn't mean that you literally dump the rest of your life in the trash. But it does mean keeping a loose grip on everything else in order to maintain a firm grip on your commitment to live passionately for Him. True surrender requires that we are ready to jettison anything—possessions, position, pedigree, popularity, preferences, people—that prevents us from living life wide open.

It's All about Being Like Jesus

But the supreme model of the passionate life of surrender is Jesus Himself. During His thirty-three years of earthly ministry, Jesus, who is in every sense the Lord of creation, subjected Himself to the will of the Father. From boyhood, Jesus's passion and purpose was to be about "My Father's business" (Luke 2:49). He kept His eyes unswerving on the goal, though He always had time for people and their needs. When He knew what faced Him in Jerusalem, He confided His emotions to God in an anguished night of prayer. The Bible tells us His grief was terrible but His surrender was total. In the end He prayed, "Father . . . nevertheless not My will, but Yours, be done" (Luke 22:42).

If you were to seek the ultimate, most passionate, most profound definition of the word *surrender,* it would read like this: "He humbled Himself and became obedient to the point of death, even the death of the cross" (Philippians 2:8). It is a surrender that rises from the passion of His love for us.

Passionate living finds its center in passionate surrender. Situation by situation, challenge by challenge, temptation by temptation, we have a choice about what to pray. We can respond by praying, in effect, "Not Your will, but mine, be done." That's not surrender; it's insurrection. And the best we can hope for is the best we can do without Christ's presence and power. Jesus was clear about the outcome of such an effort: "Without Me you can do nothing" (John 15:5).

Without Him—nothing, a life of struggle, the tension of serving two masters, and ultimate despair.

With Him—everything, a life of joy and passion, the beauty and simplicity of serving one Lord, and ultimate victory.

How can we possibly struggle to make such a choice? Join me in claiming the victory today—the victory of a war long since settled. Claim the spoils of victory, a divine inheritance the richest earthly king could not match. Simply remember to surrender—every day, every way. Then ask God to show you the way things really are in the spiritual realm, where death lies in defeat as every knee bows and every tongue confesses that Christ is Lord—and the passion of His heart, His greatest love, is *you*.

I think when you remember that truth, you'll want to build a monument for the world to see.

14

LIFE
<small>UNLEASHING *the* POWER</small>
WIDE
<small>*of a* PASSIONATE LIFE</small>
OPEN

Igniting a Passion for God

SAME OLD STORY: Mom had two sons who were driving her crazy. She had read all the parenting books. She had tried every disciplinary strategy imaginable. Her kids weren't children; they were *uncontrollable forces of nature.*

One day she was bemoaning the situation in an over-the-fence conversation with a neighbor. Her friend said, "I took my son to the pastor, and he hasn't given me a problem since."

It didn't sound like much reason to get her hopes up, but Mom had tried everything else—what did she have to lose? She marched her two sons to the car and drove them to church, where they had an appointment in the pastor's office.

The clergyman worked like a good police detective: He separated the two suspects for interrogation. The younger one waited outside while the older one faced the somber, robed minister alone. Without so much as introducing himself, the pastor stared into the eyes of the frightened boy and began his interrogation with this thundering question: "Where is God?"

The boy was speechless.

The pastor repeated, "Where is God?'

The young lad looked away, searching the room as if the answer might be found on the shelves or in a framed picture. He still kept silent. The thunder sounded closer as the minister demanded for a third time, *"Where is God?"*

This time, the boy leapt to his feet and fled the office. In the waiting room, he grabbed his brother and shouted, "Let's get out of here! They've lost God and they're trying to pin it on us!"

Have you ever lost God? Have you ever felt as if the folks at church have lost God somewhere? In my household, when something is lost, someone usually asks, "Where was the last place you had it?" For many of us, maybe that's the right question. *Where was God when I lost Him? Where did I leave Him?*

And as we reflect over those questions, we usually come to the conclusion that the last time we had God, there was a certain something in the air. There was a *feeling*. There was an energy. Perhaps the right word is *passion*. Somewhere in the course of doing life, we lost the art of feeling God. The passion drained away, and the emptiness became palpable.

In seminary, we pastors are warned about this. As a matter of fact, one of the first chapel sermons we hear is, "Don't Lose God at Seminary." In all the scholarly trappings and research papers, it's easy to become *academic* about God. Then, when we go out into the real world, we are likely to lose God again, this time in the trappings of church business and shepherding practicalities.

The idea of losing God is a terrible one. As a young minister, I was given a copy of a remarkable book called *Hudson Taylor's Spiritual Secret*. I remember writing out the statement that seemed to be the very secret promised by the title. Hudson Taylor wrote: "I saw Him, and I sought Him, and I had Him, and I wanted Him."[1]

Those fifteen words carry the whole story. All the ingredients of the conquest of life are held in those four clauses—to see, to seek, to have, and *to want*. That last part addresses this issue of losing God—will we keep wanting Him once we've found Him?

Isn't that what losing our spiritual passion is all about: losing our desire for God? That's the fourth dynamic, the one we seldom discuss. How can we explain the idea of not wanting God? How can we acknowledge such an awful truth?

A. W. Tozer wrote that the great people of the Bible and Christian history have had an insatiable hunger for God. He waits to be wanted. Too bad that with so many of us He waits so very long in vain."[2]

Desire for God is that spark that can ignite into flame or, when untended, fizzle into ashes. As we grow in the Christian life, we understand more and more that it's a fire that must be fed. Coming to know God and realizing that *He wants to be wanted* does make the flames leap within us. Think about the first time you fell in love and the object of your affection loved you back. There were two elements: your wanting and the other person's *wanting* to be wanted by you. It makes a world of difference, doesn't it? If you find that your feelings are not cherished, neither will your love last.

In the same way, we come to a place where we not only desire God but feel His pleasure, His yearning for us. There is no heart in this world that will not be touched by the realization of being cherished by the Creator of the universe. It feeds the fire of our passion, and we want Him all the more.

David describes his own passion for God: "One thing I have desired of the LORD, that will I seek: that I may dwell in the house of the LORD all the days of my life, to behold the beauty of the LORD, and to inquire in His temple" (Psalm 27:4).

David is telling us that he has one heart and one passion, and that is to know God and to be in His presence. "To inquire" is to keep seeking, to know God more and more intimately.

Psalm 42 is the classic psalm for this particular truth, and its first verse captures our desire in beautiful poetry: "As the deer pants for the water brooks, so pants my soul for You, O God. My soul thirsts for God, for the living God." This is best word picture we can imagine for the intensity of a desire for God. There is nothing more basic than the human need for water. We are the panting animal on a hot day or the exhausted athlete gasping for breath—we want Him like the water we drink and the air we breathe.

Turn to Psalm 63, and you will find it again: "O God, You are my God. Early will I seek You. My soul thirsts for You. My flesh longs for You in a dry and thirsty land where there is no water" (v. 1).

Psalm 119 holds an even more breathtaking discovery. I've never quite recovered from the impact these verses had on me when I first discovered the pattern:

- Verse 10 says we are *to seek God* with our whole heart.

- Verse 34 says we are *to observe God's Word* with our whole heart.

- Verse 40 says we are *to long after God's truth* with our whole heart.

- Verse 58 says we are *to entreat God's favor* with our whole heart.

- Verse 69 says we are *to keep God's precepts* with our whole heart.

- Verse 145 says we are *to cry unto God* with our whole heart.

The theme is as crystal-clear as the brook from which the deer drinks. *With my whole heart I will seek God.* But too often in the Christian life we stop at such generalities. We fail to explain precisely what we mean, in practical terms. This psalm spells out the precise things we must do wholeheartedly in order to seek God with that kind of passion.

A. W. Tozer had a great deal to say on passion for God, particularly in his book, *The Pursuit of God:*

Why do some persons "find" God in a way that others do not? Why does God manifest His Presence to some and let multitudes of others struggle along in the half-light of imperfect Christian experience? Of course the will of God is the same for all. He has no favorites within

His household. All He has ever done for any of His children He will do for all of His children. The difference lies not with God but with us.

Pick at random a score of great saints whose lives and testimonies are widely known. Let them be Bible characters or well known Christians of post-Biblical times. You will be struck instantly with the fact that the saints were not alike. Sometimes the unlikenesses were so great as to be positively glaring. How different for example was Moses from Isaiah; how different was Elijah from David; how unlike each other were John and Paul, St. Francis and Luther, Finney and Thomas á Kempis. The differences are as wide as human life itself: differences of race, nationality, education, temperament, habit and personal qualities. Yet they all walked, each in his day, upon a high road of spiritual living far above the common way.

Their differences must have been incidental and in the eyes of God of no significance. In some vital quality they must have been alike. What was it?

I venture to suggest that the one vital quality which they had in common was *spiritual receptivity*. Something in them was open to heaven, something which urged them Godward. Without attempting anything like a profound analysis I shall say simply that they had spiritual awareness and that they went on to cultivate it until it became the biggest thing in their lives. They differed from the average person in that when they felt the inward longing they *did something about it....* As David put it neatly, "When thou saidst, Seek ye my face; my heart said unto thee, Thy face, Lord, will I seek."[3]

My prayer is that something in me would be "open to heaven," as Tozer has described. For the truth is that we all have as much of God as we truly want.

Were you listening? Let me repeat myself: *We all have as much of God as we truly want.* I would expect (and hope) that this bit of medicine would go down like vinegar. It *should* bother us to realize that we have pursued God exactly to the point that satisfied us, and then we stopped, made camp, set out our sleeping bags, and relaxed.

Don't even attempt to say, "I want more of God. But this is as far as I've been able to go." The truth is, there is *always* more of God, and that *more* is always within reach. You can't have all of Him in one day or one week or one decade, of course—you'll never have all of Him anyway. But there is always one more touch available. Have you ever led a horse to a corral by offering him a little taste of sugar at a time, just enough to make him come forward one more step? God leads us onward with the intensity with which we are willing to come. It's a matter of how hungry we are—how much we desire that sweetness in His hand.

Our problem is that we have no idea what it means to be hungry—not like the people Jesus knew. Hunger and thirst were the twin themes of their everyday lives. If you wanted a drink, you had to walk all the way to the well—and Jesus's disciples must have had long, thirsty walks under a Middle Eastern sun. There could not have been enough water locally for the crowd at the Sermon on the Mount as Jesus said: "Blessed are they who hunger and thirst." That was *everyone*.

In a book entitled *The Romance of the Last Crusade*, Major Vivian Gilbert wrote of the thirst that he and his men suffered in the Palestinian desert during World War I, fighting their way to Jerusalem:

> Our heads ached, our eyes became blood-shot and dim in the blinding glare. Our tongues began to swell. Our lips turned to a purplish black and burst. Those who dropped out of the column were never seen again, but the desperate force battled on to Sherea. There were wells at Sherea. Had they been unable to take the place by nightfall, thousands were doomed to die of thirst. We fought that day as men fight for their lives. We entered Sherea Station on the heels of the retreating Turks. The first objects which met our view were the great stone cisterns full of cold, clear drinking water. It took four hours before the last man had his drink of water, and I believe

that we all learned our first real Bible lesson on that march from Beersheba to the Sherea wells. If such were our thirst for God and for righteousness, for his will in our lives, a consuming, all-embracing, preoccupying desire, how rich in the fruit of the Spirit we all would be.[4]

Sadly, most of us are not fighting our way to Jerusalem, our tongues parched for God. We have no desire to feel anything so uncomfortable—the more padding in the pew cushion, the better. We build our churches today on the twin pillars of convenience and comfort. We don't really go in for that "fanaticism" trip. No, we like all things in moderation, balancing work and hobbies and friends and God.

Could that be the reason we've lost Him? Could it be that it's necessary to feel intense, parched-throat, black-tongued thirst before we capture in our soul the true taste of the living water? Could it be that our stomach must be empty, that we must ache and feel faint for want of God before we can truly taste the miracle of the bread of life?

Jesus said that people are blessed when they hunger and thirst after righteousness. Let's explore some of the realities of true spiritual hunger.

SOME SPIRITUAL HUNGER IS THE REALITY OF YOUR FAITH

In one way, Jesus's statement about hunger and thirst is somber and demanding; yet in another, it touchingly shows the gentleness of His compassion. Yes, Jesus is giving us the condition demanded of our soul. But on the other hand, He is reassuring us that we will be blessed by God in the struggle and the seeking. To find God, we must yearn for Him very deeply. But in the yearning, in the midst of our tears, we feel the touch of His hand on our shoulder.

If Jesus had said, "Blessed are those who attain righteousness," there would be nobody to be blessed. Instead, He says to us, in essence:

Blessed are the pilgrims who wander in the wilderness yet keep dreaming of Canaan.

Blessed are the disciples who fail to walk on water yet keep getting out of the boat.

Blessed are the foul-ups, the dropouts, and the wanna-bes who keep getting up off the floor.

What He says is that we'll never totally succeed; we'll always be wanting. But God will be smiling upon us.

It is the heart that moves God to bless us. Later in the Sermon, Jesus said that our heart condemns us when we hate or lust inwardly, even when we do the right things on the outside. Here it is just the reverse: In the Beatitudes, Jesus talks about those people who are failing and struggling and being persecuted but keep the fire alive within their heart. Blessed are they.

Martyn Lloyd-Jones said:

This Beatitude follows logically from the previous one. It is a statement to which all others lead. It is the logical conclusion to which they come. It is something for which we should be profoundly thankful and grateful to God. I do not know of a better test that anyone can apply to himself in this whole matter of the Christian profession than a verse like this. . . . If this verse is to you one of the most blessed statements in the whole Scripture, you can be quite sure you are a Christian. If it is not, you better examine your foundations again.[5]

The issue, in other words, is not that we aren't all that we could be; the issue is that we don't really *want* to be. We have as much of God as we want. Just as long as we have that ticket punched to heaven, as long as the sermons don't run too long, as long as we can fall back on prayer when nothing else works, as long as the facilities are nice at church, as long as Jesus provides comfort without demands—*we have all of Him that we want.*

"Blessed are those who hunger and thirst for righteousness" (Matthew 5:6) is the spiritual barometer in your Bible, as Martyn Lloyd-Jones said. If you know exactly what that verse is talking about, congratulations; you're a child of God. Maybe you don't know God as well as you could, but it bothers you. That *bother* is the gentle prodding of the Holy Spirit.

SPIRITUAL HUNGER IS THE REQUIREMENT FOR YOUR GROWTH

There is another little test Jesus applied—another barometer. One day, as recorded in Matthew 19, Jesus came across a rich young man who told Him about his passion for heaven. Jesus told the man to keep the commandments, and the man quickly replied that he'd kept them all his life. So Jesus looked at him again and said, "Go and sell everything and give it to the poor." At this point the rich young man turned his eyes to his feet and his feet to the horizon. He had as much of Jesus, he discovered, as he really wanted.

Surely most of us would fail the same test. Is the issue about selling our possessions? No, it's an issue of passion. Jesus wanted to see the man's eyes when he heard what the Lord was asking him to do. For you or me, the question might be a different one. What God is looking for is hunger, thirst, true yearning. It's the precious pearl someone would sell everything to own, the one thing we would cling to if everything else were snatched away.

There is another saying of Jesus I have a vivid picture of Him delivering. He is walking through the town at the height of His fame, surrounded by a crowd, the din of all the shouts and cries, the jostling and grabbing, the shoving and maneuvering—the scene is chaos. From the eye of the storm, Jesus sees all the commotion. He hears all the demands and says, in a commanding voice, "Wait! Before you follow Me, let Me tell you, if you are not willing to deny yourselves and leave family and home . . ." And He speaks of leaving the plow in the middle of the field, leaving the dead to bury the dead, leaving *everything,* just like *that.*

As they say on television, *now* how much would you pay?

The price is our passion—full, unmitigated, thirsty passion.

The Lack of Spiritual Hunger Is the Reason for Your Spiritual Failure

If we fail to find all that we want of Christ, it is not because He is unavailable. It has been said that most of the things we *really* want, we get; that the true prayers of the innermost heart are always answered, but the key is to be aware what your innermost heart is really saying. If you want to be married, there are ways. If you want to get into college, there are ways. If you want to make a million dollars, it's not as impossible as you think. It's all in the *want to.* There are incredibly gifted athletes who fail and untalented ones who make it to the highest level.

But God is attainable to every single member of the human race. Again, it's a matter of the *want to.*

Consider Paul, who had three visions of Christ in his lifetime. In 2 Corinthians 12 he described how he was caught up into the third heaven and saw things that were beyond his human vocabulary. Paul had a remarkable physical life and a remarkable spiritual life. How touching it is that in his final years, when he knew the end was coming, he wrote that he had only one desire, which he hadn't yet fulfilled:

That I may know Him and the power of His resurrection, and the fellowship of His sufferings, being conformed to His death, if, by any means, I may attain to the resurrection from the dead. Not that I have already attained, or am already perfected; but I press on, that I may

158

lay hold of that for which Christ Jesus has also laid hold of me.
Brethren, I do not count myself to have apprehended; but one thing I
do, forgetting those things which are behind and reaching forward to
those things which are ahead, I press toward the goal for the prize of
the upward call of God in Christ Jesus. (Philippians 3:10–14)

Here was a man exalted by the early church, obviously admired
by all his correspondents. And he was telling them that he had one
goal and he hadn't reached it. The older he got, the closer he got,
and the more he wanted to lay hold of that for which he'd been laid
hold of.

I long to be that kind of man when I stand on the outskirts of this
short life. I long to be uncomfortable, not settled into an easy-chair
faith in an easy-chair church, surrounded by people who reassure
me that we've reached the bonus rounds of the kingdom of God, so
we can just put up our feet and watch the world go by. No, I choose
to be like Paul and live thirsty—straining to take hold of the prize,
knowing I'll never quite get my fingertips on it in this life. The
straining hurts, but it's a *good* kind of hurt—a *blessed* kind of hurt.

The question is, Do you want to be comfortable or Christlike,
relaxed or renewed?

If you want to be Christlike, ask yourself whether you are satisfied. The Puritans used to say, "He has the most need of righteousness who least wants it." They were right about that. Are you
smug, self-satisfied, and feeling pretty good about where you are
spiritually? If that's your feeling, then you aren't hungry.

Do you have an appetite for the Word of God? Jeremiah the
prophet said, "Thy words were found, and I ate them" (Jeremiah
15:16). The Word is our food, and a living, invigorated spirit
hungers for more and more food. Sherwood Elliot Wirt, former
editor of *Decision,* explained:

The problem with this whole hunger issue with Christians is that
often we think spiritual hunger works the same way physical hunger

159

works. When you are physically hungry, the longer you go without eating, the hungrier you get. When you finally do eat, fill yourself up, your hunger is satisfied. In the spiritual realm, it's exactly the opposite of that. In the spiritual realm, the longer you go without eating, the more your appetite wanes. If you don't eat, you can go for long periods of time and you aren't even hungry."[6]

It works in reverse too. Physically, the more you eat, the more you're full; eating satisfies your hunger. But spiritually, the more you're filled with the Word, the more you want; spiritual appetite only intensifies. No one truly experiences God and says, "That'll do me for a couple of weeks." The more you have of Him, the more you want of Him.

Sometimes, of course, we hit the depths. It takes passion to restore passion, and our needle is on empty. We pick up the Bible, and it's as dry as dust. The sermons don't come to life. Prayer life is nonexistent. Like the two boys in the church, we've lost God. It is in these times that we should use the strategy I call "force-feeding," based on the principle that it's better to act your way into feeling than to try feeling your way into acting.

Mothers with small children know what I'm talking about. Or perhaps you've had to take medicine that tastes wretched. If you're wise, you take your medicine even when it doesn't taste good. In the same way, sit down. Open your Bible. Read. If drowsiness beckons, read aloud. Stay the course. Sooner or later—this comes with my guarantee—God is going to show up again. I assure you, you'll know when it happens. It will be like rain after a long drought, feasting after days of starvation. It will feel as if a door has opened in your heart, and springtime sunshine is flooding in.

The next day, you'll show up for Bible reading ten minutes early, and you'll go overtime. And as passion for God steals back into your life, an amazing thing will happen. All the passions of your heart will begin to fall into place, to seek their proper levels. You'll realize that it was more than spiritual dryness that was besetting your soul. When you lose Him, you lose everything. And it is only when He is once again rediscovered that you realize the proper place of every other passion and concern.

I hope you never lose God. But if you do, remember that He doesn't withhold His blessing from those of us who wander along the road—as long as we're pointed toward heaven, passionately seeking, hungry, thirsty, and wide open for the homeward journey.

15

LIFE
UNLEASHING *the* POWER
WIDE
of a PASSIONATE LIFE
OPEN

Keep the Fire Burning

JACK LALANNE is a name you may remember. Often called the "Godfather of Fitness," he opened the first modern health spa in the United States in 1936. Then, in 1951, he sparked the first fitness craze through his exercise show on television.

At this writing, I was surprised to discover that Jack LaLanne is still going strong in his late eighties. As a matter of fact, he and his wife, Elaine, stay busy traveling all over the world, offering motivational speeches and fitness advice. He's not too keen on the idea of retiring to an easy chair and living off soap operas. Somehow, the fire inside him just won't extinguish.

When LaLanne turned seventy, he celebrated his birthday by towing seventy boats containing seventy people for a mile across Long Beach Harbor. But he didn't want anyone to think he was taking it too easy, so he added one more twist. LaLanne towed the boats by holding the rope in his teeth while handcuffed and wearing leg shackles.

Picture this septuagenarian towing seventy boats, rope in his mouth, chains on his hands and feet. How would you like to be capable of that kind of stunt on your seventieth birthday?

There's something we notice about high achievers. They never retire; the fire in their belly simply doesn't let them slow down. This

163

is doubly true of God's top servants. Study the life of any of the men and women who have had a profound impact for God, and you'll see they were as active as ever right up to the last day God gave them on this planet. Billy Graham has often remarked that the Lord doesn't give retirement parties and gold watches—and these soldiers of the gospel wouldn't have it any other way because the passion burns intensely within them.

FIVE WAYS TO KEEP THE FIRE BURNING

I know you're like me—you want to go out with a bang, not a whimper. But if we struggle to keep the passion alive now, how can we do so for a lifetime? Let's explore how we can keep those flames stoked.

1. *Stretch beyond your comfort zone.* John F. Kennedy once said, "Only those who dare to fail miserably can achieve greatly." Fear and hesitation are among the first factors that will douse the passion within you. If you worry about failure or overextending, you'll retire meekly back into that comfort zone, and next time it will be harder to emerge and push out your boundaries.

Unfortunately, we often *encourage* comfort zones in the church. Calvin Miller noticed the underlying message in many of our hymns:

> We huddle in the cleft of the rock to avoid the storms, not to stand on the craggy heights and let them exhilarate us. I was struck one day by all the hymns that center on faith as a protective refuge: "O Safe to the Rock That Is Higher Than I"; "Haven of Rest"; "I Have Found a Hiding Place"; . . . "The Solid Rock"; "Hold the Fort for I Am Coming"; "Under His Wings I Am Safely Abiding"; "Jesus Is a Rock in a Weary Land"; "Rock of Ages, Cleft for Me"; "A Mighty Fortress Is Our God"; to name a few.[1]

We should sing more about the full armor of God. We should be shouting, "Onward, Christian Soldiers" and rallying behind spiritual march anthems rather than comfort music for weak-kneed saints. Perhaps we need Jack LaLanne to tell us, "Stretch!" For that's where the adventure lies. Stretch beyond your limits.

But what if you hold back? Time passes, and twenty years from now you will be more disappointed by the things you didn't do than by the things you did. Talk to an elderly saint and he's likely to tell you that if he had it to do all over again, he would take more risks and less shelter. It's a day-by-day choice. Charge forward or retreat and hide? T. S. Eliot said, "Only those who risk going too far can possibly find out how far one can go."

Just be forewarned that risk is—well, *risky*. I won't tell you that your courage and daring will guarantee that you won't fail, because I've learned another thing about high achievers: They fail quite often before their big breakthroughs. What if you knew you could earn fifty million dollars, but first you would have to start ten businesses and fail in them, one by one? Would you do it? I believe most people, given those terms, would consider the prize worth the stumbles.

No, this isn't about money. It's about acknowledging the possibility of failure and pushing on anyway, knowing what the reward will be. It's about tenacity and perseverance. In the end, the storyline is not who among us stumbled but who got up from the ground one more time. That person is the one who wins the race and the prize that Paul described in 1 Corinthians 9.

Ask yourself what holds you back from taking risks. Is it fear? Think in terms of the challenge laid before you, and ask yourself about the worst-case scenario. Is the risk really so terrible? Perhaps you'll conclude that regret from not moving forward is the worst that can happen. And know this: Each time you show courage and take the risk, you gain confidence and experience that will embolden you for the next time; each time you shy away, you drain yourself of boldness and passion.

Passionate people are always "pushing the envelope," in the words of Chuck Yeager, the first pilot to break the sound barrier. They are looking to see where the line in the sand has been drawn—

the line no one else will push a toe past. Passionate people have restless toes!

Sure, there are risks not worth taking. Don't risk your family or your health. Don't risk your life to see if you can jump over the Grand Canyon in a motorcycle, as Evel Knievel did. But I think you realize those aren't the risks we're discussing. I find that most people will not risk attaining their heart's desire because they're afraid of losing what doesn't satisfy them anyway. What are you hanging onto? Is it worth the sacrifice of great adventure?

At halftime of a football game, the coach of the losing team laid down a two-by-four in the middle of the locker room—a plain wooden plank you'd use for building a house. He asked his team to line up and walk the plank. They looked at him as if he was crazy, but they did it. Afterward, the coach said, "Now, how many of you would walk across that same plank if I took it off the floor and suspended it between the windows of two buildings on the fiftieth floor?" No hands were raised.

The coach explained that the difference is in the power of fear, the intimidation of risk. Every single team member could walk across that two-by-four when it was on the ground—and they could do so no less easily fifty floors higher. The difference is only in *perception.*

God cares a lot about our perception. He wants us to stop taking counsel of our fears and cross the Jordan into the land of promise He has for each of us. The Israelites were within eleven days' walk of Canaan for thirty-eight years—it was a matter not of crossing a plank but of crossing a river. A generation died with their hopes unrealized because they could not stop thinking of the giants in the land.

The generation before mine didn't like risk; they had known too much suffering while growing up during the Great Depression and living in the shadow of Hitler and totalitarianism. After coming through the nightmare, what that generation valued more than anything in the world was security—freedom from fear and risk. They wanted to work hard, live in one house, and hold one job until retirement. Nothing seemed more attractive than security and predictability. Unfortunately, my generation has inherited that mind-set.

I once fit neatly into that category until I found out I had cancer. Talk about a wake-up call! I suddenly realized that life is short, that every day God gives me is precious, and that living a life of passion, even in the shadow of uncertainty, is worth it. I don't wish to die until I've really lived, so I have renewed my commitment to push the envelope for Christ by living wide open for Him every day I have left.

I'm profoundly thankful to God that my cancer is in remission as I write these words. But it could return at any time. I wake up every morning committed to practice the art of wholehearted living by rushing boldly ahead to accomplish what I can. What's the point of holding back and playing it safe?

So I do my "stretching" exercises every day. I stretch myself toward more passion in family life, toward more passion in ministry, toward more passion in every direction. And I find that when I stretch, it brings everything else in my life into perspective. Pushing the envelope enhances the experience of being passionately alive.

2. *Spend time with kids.* The next time you walk out of a passion-sapping committee meeting at work or at church, find the nearest five-year-old. What you need is a healthy dose of innocence and vitality. No one is more filled with wide-open passion than children. Have you ever seen a little boy catching fireflies dispassionately? Have you ever seen a little girl whose eyes didn't sparkle when she told you about her dolls?

Children wake up excited in the morning, and they fight bedtime because the vitality is still bubbling in them. They can still think of fifty perfectly good uses for this day, so why have bedtime at all?

We can take a cue from children by asking lots of questions, laughing as often as possible, and never walking anywhere we're allowed to run. If you lived this way, other adults would look at you suspiciously at first. Then it would occur to them that you've found something to be excited about, something to learn, somewhere to run. People would say, "Finally, someone who has fifty perfectly good uses for this day!"

We don't want to be childish, but we do want to be childlike. Remember, Jesus held up little children as examples of faith: "Then Jesus called a little child to Him, set him in the midst of them, and said, 'Assuredly, I say to you, unless you are converted and become as little children, you will by no means enter the kingdom of heaven. Therefore whoever humbles himself as this little child is the greatest in the kingdom of heaven'" (Matthew 18:2–4). Their gift is in seeing life in its simplicity rather than making everything complicated.

3. *Seek out exciting experiences.* Passion is sustained in our heart by the experiences we have in life. We have proven this over the years at Shadow Mountain Community Church. During the late eighties I began to feel a great burden within me concerning foreign missions. My burden grew out of a visit to the mission fields of Guatemala and Peru. During my visit, I was invited to attend retirement parties for long-term missionaries who were leaving their tours of duty and heading back to the States for the final time.

As these missionaries spoke about their time on the mission field, they all wept as they talked about leaving their ministries. Leaving it all behind was tough, but the worst part by far was the hard truth that no one had been found to replace them on the field of service. I remember feeling tears well up as I looked at the weathered faces of these veteran missionaries with no one coming behind them. They had exchanged their lives for their work, and what would come of it?

When I returned to San Diego, I was in a hurry to tell this story to our church. My heart was beating rapidly as I asked our people to agree on a goal to place two hundred career missionaries on the field by the year 2000. I worked to make our church passionate about missions, and I'm happy to report that we reached and surpassed that goal. We gave God the glory, for He answered our prayer.

From the human perspective, however, there was a secret. On

more than one occasion I had read this statistic: One-fourth of all short-term missionaries return to the field as full-time career missionaries. I remember challenging our people with this statistic and telling them that if we were going to reach our goal of two hundred career missionaries on the field by the year 2000, we would have to get eight hundred short-term missionaries to the field.

During the next couple of years, we sent more than eight hundred of our people on short-term missionary trips, and the statistic proved to be accurate. What was the secret? It was the experience of our people seeing firsthand what mission work was all about. Many of them had given money for missions in the past. But after short-term missions, they were ready to give their heart and life.

As this book is being written, several of our radio and television staff have just returned from Honduras and Caracas, Venezuela, where we held our first-ever radio rallies on foreign soil. I preached through an interpreter, and we saw many people come to Christ as the gospel was presented. When we returned from that experience, every one of us was changed. Our passion for what God was doing through our Spanish radio program was fanned into a brightly burning flame.

I'm so grateful for the firsthand experiences I'm able to have, because they change me.

4. *Surround yourself with passionate people.* Passion is contagious. We give off sparks of excitement and energy, and those sparks alight in someone else. Conversely, I learned early in ministry that I could not afford the luxury of being exposed to people who demotivated me. I've learned to take care whom I'm around because of what I can catch from them.

It was exactly one year after winning the Olympic gold medal that Eric Liddell went to China as a missionary with the London Missionary Society. By bicycle and by foot, he carried the gospel of Jesus Christ to the back country of China, building on the foundation Hudson Taylor had left.

After Japan invaded China and World War II broke out, Liddell was classified as an "enemy national," and in August 1943 he was sent to a prison camp. He was one of eighteen hundred prisoners packed into a facility that measured 150 by 200 yards. He was housed in a dormitory that provided a room three feet by six feet for each man. While a prisoner, Liddell accepted the challenge of his situation and organized athletic meets, taught hymns, and ministered God's Word.

David Mitchell was a child who was interred along with Eric Liddell. He later remembered the influence this national hero had upon everyone in the prison. He said, "None of us will ever forget this man who was totally committed to putting God first, a man whose humble life combined muscular Christianity with radiant godliness."[2]

Just months before he would have been liberated, on February 21, 1945, Eric Liddell died of a brain tumor. What was it about Liddell that had such a great impact on David Mitchell? Here is the answer to that question in David Mitchell's own words: "What was his secret? He unreservedly committed his life to Jesus Christ as Savior and Lord. That friendship meant everything to him. By the flickering light of a peanut-oil lamp, early each morning, he and a roommate in the men's dormitory studied the Bible and talked with God for an hour. As a Christian, Eric Liddell's desire was to know God more deeply, and as a missionary, to make Him known more fully."[3]

God is always looking for someone available, whether in a Chinese prison or in your own neighborhood—and sometimes from the most unlikely places. Not long ago we met to plan a men's ministry in our church. The first thing we needed was a men's minister. We received résumés from men who'd been involved in similar ministries in other churches. We interviewed and kept searching, but a good man proved hard to find.

Meanwhile, one of our own members was being released from prison. In the past, he had committed some serious business errors, but he did the right thing by turning himself in when he discovered what had happened. John came to see me and described how God had changed his life and his heart while he was in prison. He said that he had absolutely no desire to return to the world of business; he and his wife, Lisa, wanted to devote the rest of their lives to serving Jesus Christ.

Here was a man who had been surrounded by men and their needs during his sentence. He had developed an intense passion for discipling men and watching them grow. He also had the painful wisdom that comes from the folly of building a life strictly around business and money. He had quite a message for businessmen everywhere. As we talked, the sparks seemed to leap out of him and into me. His passion was contagious; I hadn't had this feeling about any candidate we had interviewed for our men's ministry leader. I asked John if he would be interested in being considered for that position, and immediately he became animated and excited.

You can tell where this story is going. By now, John has set the men of our church on fire. His passion continues to start brush fires among the businessmen of San Diego.

By the way, there were those who wrote letters advising us not to hire a "felon" on a church staff. But I knew God's track record with the prodigal sons who have always filled the ranks of His army.

Like John, difference-makers in ministry are always people of passion. They exude an enthusiasm that inspires followers. I have to tell most of them to take time off, to go home at night, to spend time with their family. They live and breathe their life's passion, and they hate bedtime! We want our ministers to feel that it's not a job but an adventure.

5. *See the big picture.* Passionate people see beyond the temporal to the eternal. They dream big, knowing that God is always up to something. As long as this world continues to spin, God will be working through people like you and me. He will be implanting dreams and visions in people—dreams and visions that bring the world closer to His own visions. Nothing happens until people begin to see the world as God sees it—unlimited by time or space but governed by eternal purposes.

171

You might say, "That sounds great, but I'm just a little person. I'm no visionary. What difference could I make?" Know that the size of your particular role is not important. It's the size of your dream for your role that counts.

In her poem "Hold Fast Your Dreams," early twentieth-century poet Louise Driscoll eloquently captured the power and purpose of our dreams:

> Hold fast your dreams!
> Within your heart
> Keep one still, secret spot
> Where dreams may go,
> And, sheltered so,
> May thrive and grow
> Where doubt and fear are not.
> Oh keep a place apart,
> Within your heart,
> For little dreams to go!
>
> Think still of lovely things that are not true.
> Let wish and magic work at will in you.
> Be sometimes blind to sorrow. Make believe!
> Forget the calm that lies
> In disillusioned eyes.
> Though we all know that we must die,
> Yet you and I may walk like gods and be
> Even now at home in immortality.
>
> We see so many ugly things—
> Deceits and wrongs and quarrelings;
> We know, alas! we know
> How quickly fade
> The color in the west,

The bloom upon the flower,
The bloom upon the breast
And youth's blind hour.
Yet keep within your heart
A place apart
Where little dreams may go,
May thrive and grow.
Hold fast—hold fast your dreams!

What dream beats within your heart? What would a life wide open look like for you?

MAKING IT HAPPEN

Passionate people begin by seeing castles in the air. Then they start to build the stairway.

Before the journey begins, there must be concrete goals. Where are you going? How are you going to get there? By when? What are the steps on the stairway, and in what order? You pray, you draw as near to God as possible, and you trust Him to inspire the best plans possible.

All the while, of course, you remember that there will be periods of three steps forward, two steps back. There will be bursts of full-steam-ahead and complete breakdowns. "A man's heart plans his way, but the LORD directs his steps" (Proverbs 16:9). Your plan is a subset of God's plan, and you can be certain that what seems like a failure or a setback for you is still, always, eternally something He will use in His grand design (see Romans 8:28). That's why it's so crucial to be a big picture-thinker.

But setbacks and all, you're on the journey of a lifetime. Passion is your fuel. Dreams are your navigator's wheel. When you leave the land of predictability, your passion will never die; the fire will never go out because you'll be living on adrenaline. You launch

173

forward and set a course for eternity. What was it Peter Pan said as he launched into the sky? "Second star to the right, and straight on 'til morning!"

Yes, there are going to be risks. Yes, there will be moments when you question your own sanity for having set out. But you know in your heart you're doing the right thing. This is what God has been calling you to do, and it feels great to be doing it—it feels *passionate.*

It feels like a life wide open, so let's start living it *today.*

LIFE
UNLEASHING *the* POWER
WIDE
of a PASSIONATE LIFE
OPEN

Wide Open All the Way

WHEN DR. J. VERNON MCGEE talked about the Bible,
people listened. He was the most beloved Bible teacher of
his generation.

My church was the site of his last public sermon, and I was
afforded the thrill of spending two hours with him. What would
you expect a man of declining health to talk about? The past? The
good old days? Not Dr. McGee. The only subject that interested
him was the future. He was fascinated by the technology of audio-
tape and broadcasting, which would keep his ministry fruitful long
after he was gone.

He was correct about that. Fifteen years after Dr. McGee's
death, the *Wall Street Journal* published an article about him.
Writer Anna Wilde Matthews reported that McGee's radio
program was broadcast on eight hundred stations in the U.S. and
Canada. His teachings were being beamed around the world via
satellite and the Internet in more than one hundred languages. *Thru
the Bible,* his radio program, has added three hundred North
American affiliates and dozens of new languages since his death in
1988. Dr. McGee's wholehearted ministry has not stopped even for
his death.

It's fascinating that Dr. McGee foresaw this and carefully

planted the seeds for it. In his final recorded message, he was preaching from the verse: "By faith Abel offered to God a more excellent sacrifice than Cain, through which he obtained witness that he was righteous, God testifying of his gifts; *and through it he being dead still speaks*" (Hebrews 11:4; emphasis added). In other words, the excellence of his gifts gave him a voice from beyond the grave. That's what Dr. McGee wanted, and again God has granted it.[1] Some men leave monuments of stone, but I'd much rather leave a living monument that continues to write itself into the hearts of millions of people. What greater legacy could there be?

Though he spoke of Cain, Dr. J. Vernon McGee reminds me more of Caleb, the less celebrated friend of Joshua. You'll remember that the two of them brought the minority report from the Promised Land, which they described as an abundant land of milk and honey. They were ready to seize their inheritance in God's name. But the other scouts—the majority party—counseled the Israelites to fear the giants in the land and keep away. The lack of faith cost Israel an entire generation of restless wandering before they finally claimed the land God had reserved for them.

But are you familiar with the rest of Caleb's story? He was eighty-five years old when he achieved his peak accomplishment— a man living with wide-open faith until the end, just like J. Vernon McGee.

ENTHUSIASTIC ABOUT LIFE

This is how Caleb described himself at age eighty-five: "And now, behold, the LORD has kept me alive, as He said, these forty-five years, ever since the LORD spoke this word to Moses while Israel wandered in the wilderness; and now, here I am this day, eighty-five years old. As yet I am as strong this day as on the day that Moses sent me, just as my strength was then, so now is my strength for war, both for going out and for coming in" (Joshua 14:10–11).

It's clear that Caleb was passionate in his youth as well as his elderly years, but where did his passion come from? It certainly wasn't the product of an easy journey. You could summarize Caleb's life at eighty-five in three Ds: desert, death, and discouragement.

All his contemporaries were dying. You might remember that a condition for entering the Promised Land was that all of the unfaithful generation—the one that shied away from giants—had to die before God would permit the crossing of the Jordan. It took thirty-eight wilderness years for that to happen. Caleb grew older as he waited through the decades, checking the obituaries every day and seeing the last of his old friends die.

A generation of funerals would make the best of us gloomy and morose. But not Caleb. The verses above show that his engines were still revving. The fire in the furnace of his soul was still lit. He was still living wide open for God.

EXCITED ABOUT THE FUTURE

Several years ago, Lee Eisenberg wrote these words about nine secular leaders who had distinguished themselves by their vision: "While their contemporaries groped at the present to feel a pulse, or considered the past to discern the course that led to the moment, these nine squinted through the veil of the future. Not that they were mystics. . . . For most of them, reality was pure and simple. What set them apart was the conviction that a greater reality lay a number of years down the pike."[2]

No one questioned Caleb's pulse. Forty years earlier he had done reconnaissance work in hostile territory. He and Joshua had seen opportunity where the others had seen opposition. He based his recommendations not on the problems but on the provision and power of God. Listen to the boldness in his declaration: "Caleb quieted the people before Moses, and said, 'Let us go up at once and take possession, for we are well able to overcome it. . . .' And they spoke to all the congregation of the children of Israel, saying, 'The land we passed through to spy out is an exceedingly good land. If the Lord delights in us, then He will bring us into this land and give it to us, a land which flows with milk and honey'" (Numbers 13:30; 14:7–8).

Oh, if only the people had listened to the voice of faith instead of the voice of fear. In taking counsel of the latter, they doomed themselves to a generation of emptiness and wandering. And so we do the same when we listen to the wrong internal voices.

Caleb waited out the time though the punishment wasn't his to endure. He kept his heart young and his faith active, and at eighty-five years old he told God what he wanted: "Now therefore, give me this mountain of which the Lord spoke in that day; for you heard in that day how the Anakim were there, and that the cities were great and fortified. It may be that the LORD will be with me, and I shall be able to drive them out as the LORD said" (Joshua 14:12).

What would most of us have asked for at eighty-five? "Lord, give me a nice mountain cabin in one of the fortified regions, where I'll be safe. Just give me a nice place to rest these tired bones." Who would have criticized Caleb for being ready to take it easy? We expect people to be broken down and living in quiet despair by that age.

In his book *The Fifth Discipline*, Peter Senge quoted Bill O'Brien, CEO of Hanover Insurance: "People enter business as bright, well educated, high energy people, full of desire to make a difference. By the time they are 30, a few are on the fast track and the rest put in their time and do what really matters to them on the weekend. They lose the commitment, the sense of mission, and the excitement with which they started their careers. We get . . . little of their energy and almost none of their spirit."[3]

Senge went on to explain what happens to people as they get older and lose their vision and passion:

> Most adults have little sense of real vision. We have goals and objec-
> tives, but these are not visions. When asked what they want, many
> adults will say what they want to get rid of. They'd like a better
> job—that is, they'd like to get rid of the boring job they have. They'd

like to live in a better neighborhood, or not have to worry about crime, or about putting their kids through school. They'd like it if their mother-in-law returned to her own house, or if their back stopped hurting. Such litanies of "negative visions" are sadly commonplace, even among very successful people. . . . As a teenager in one of our programs once said, "We shouldn't call them 'grown ups,' we should call them 'given ups.'"[4]

According to Senge, the lack of passion leaves you with "little energy and no spirit." Do you know a few people who fall into this category? I hope it's not true of you. I would rather be a Caleb. He did not use his gray hair to beg off the heavy lifting. He asked for a worthy challenge because he had the wisdom to know that with powerful quest comes powerful reward. Knock down a giant, and you become one yourself.

Of course, the alternative is to live this way:

> Since I retired from life's competition,
> Each day is filled with complete repetition.
> I get up each morning and dust off my wits,
> Go pick up the paper and read the "obits."
> If my name isn't there, I know I'm not dead,
> So I get a good breakfast and go back to bed.

We might call that a life shut tight, and I'll let someone else write *that* book. My models are Caleb and J. Vernon McGee, who give me hope that old age isn't something to dread.

Calvin Miller, in his book *Into the Depths of God,* reflected on his own passion:

So often these days I am caught trying to figure out what daring things I still have the courage to do. When I was younger, no roller coaster ever intimidated me, no precipitous hike seemed too dangerous. I once dived off a seventy-foot waterfall. I have hiked the

Grand Canyon at night, rafted the Mendenhall river in Alaska and the Rio Grande through the Box at Taos, New Mexico. Now I consider those things I still haven't done and yet want to do. I have recently climbed partway up Ayres Rock in the Outback of Australia, hiked some distance along the Great Wall, taken a helicopter ride over Mount Rushmore, parasailed around the Gulf of Mexico, and ridden "The Rattler" at Astro World.[5]

Why is it that we fear growing old? Proverbs 16:31 tells us, "The silver-haired head is a crown of glory," but our youth-obsessed culture has taught us to consider it a thorny crown indeed.

The truth is that as soon as we stop living, we begin dying.

ENERGIZED BY HIS ASSIGNMENT

We find the words "old and advanced in years" six times in the Bible. It means exactly what it says. But is there a hidden meaning? Five of the six times this phrase crops up in the Bible, the "old, advanced" person is about to experience something astounding.

Abraham (one hundred years old) and Sarah (age ninety) are "old and advanced in years" as they are about to give birth to Isaac. Zacharias and Elizabeth are "old and advanced in years" before they give birth to John the Baptist. And we're told that Joshua, too, is "old and advanced in years" before he receives his marching orders to enter the land of God's promise.

The Israelites were given specific instructions about dealing with the region's inhabitants. But at age eighty-five, only Caleb fully carried out his orders. As we read through these chapters in Joshua, we see the words "did not drive them out" over and over—a litany of failure:

- Nevertheless the children of Israel did not drive out the Geshurites or the Maachathites, but the Geshurites and the Maachathites dwell among the Israelites until this day (Joshua 13:13).

- As for the Jebusites, the inhabitants of Jerusalem, the children of Judah could not drive them out, but the Jebusites dwell with the children of Judah at Jerusalem to this day (Joshua 15:63).

- And they did not drive out the Canaanites who dwelt in Gezer; but the Canaanites dwell among the Ephraimites to this day and have become forced laborers (Joshua 16:10).

After the glorious crossing of the Jordan, the Israelites left unfinished business in their wake. If they had driven out the various tribes who were enemies of God, their future would have been peaceful and secure. Instead, the Canaanites remained a thorn in Israel's collective side for years to come.

But then there was Caleb: "Caleb drove out the three sons of Anak from there, Sheshai, Ahiman, and Talmai, the children of Anak" (Joshua 15:14). No unfinished business there. Caleb did exactly what he was told, and he did it immediately. He is one of those success stories whose secret is not so secret. That is, when we look at high achievers, we can often quickly isolate the distinctive that set them apart.

In Caleb's case, thirty verses hold his entire life story in the Scriptures. And six times in those thirty verses we see a recurring theme:

- But my servant Caleb—this is a different story. He has a different spirit; he follows me passionately. I'll bring him into the land that he scouted and his children will inherit it (Numbers 14:24 MSG).

- None, except for Caleb son of Jephunneh the Kenizzite, and Joshua son of Nun followed me—their hearts were in it (Numbers 32:12 MSG).

- Not a single person of this evil generation is going to get so much as a look at the good land that I promised to give to

181

your parents. Not one—except for Caleb son of Jephunneh. He'll see it. I'll give him and his descendants the land he walked on because he was all for following God, heart and soul (Deuteronomy 1:35–36 MSG).

- My companions who went with me discouraged the people, but I stuck to my guns, totally with God, my God. That was the day Moses solemnly promised, "The land on which your feet have walked will be our inheritance, you and your children's forever. Yes, you have lived totally for God" (Joshua 14:8–9 MSG).

- Hebron belongs to Caleb son of Jephunneh the Kenizzite still today, because he gave himself totally to God, the God of Israel (Joshua 14:14 MSG).

Caleb's passion breaks through so we can't miss it. He had a "different spirit" and followed God with all his heart. The Great Commandment was embedded deep in Caleb's soul in his early life, and it guided him throughout all his days. By the time he was eighty-five, while most of his generation had given up hope and died, Caleb still had a bright fire burning. He still wanted to leap on the greatest possible task that God could give him.

Modern Calebs do still walk the earth—I can name a trio of them quickly. I spoke at a conference in the Carolinas where George Beverly Shea, ninety-four years young, gave a one-hour concert. My wife and I were privileged to share dinner and conversation with the Sheas, and their wholehearted love of God shone forth.

As I write this book, we have just finished the Billy Graham mission in San Diego. On three different occasions I was with Dr. Graham as we prayed together and talked about the mission. At eighty-four, he is still passionate about evangelism; he continues to preach with vibrancy and effectiveness. He serves God wholeheartedly, and he'll do so until the Lord calls him home.

Cliff Barrows, eighty, is the youngster of these three wise men. As Dr. Graham's longtime friend, he still leads the congregational singing and serves as the host at the rallies. He and his wife are filled with a beautiful spirit of Christian grace.

In his biography of Bob Pierce, Dr. Graham's son Franklin tells about Dr. Charles McCoy, a pastor in Oyster Bay, New York. Dr. McCoy was a tall, distinguished man with seven university degrees. His church expected him to step down at age seventy-two and move into a retirement home. But Dr. McCoy was an explorer at heart, and to everyone's surprise, he sold his possessions and traveled to India, where a man had invited him to preach. His friends tried to dissuade him, saying, "You might die in India." But he replied, "It's just as close to heaven from there as it is from here." During his trip, his luggage was lost, and he no sooner arrived in India than his billfold and passport were stolen.

The man who had invited him had returned to the States, and Dr. McCoy knew no one else in India. A group of missionaries took him in but weren't sure what to do with him. Dr. McCoy never missed a beat. He traveled through Asia for sixteen years, having unusual opportunities to share Christ before political leaders, military academies, educational institutions, and large crowds of humanity. He planted churches in Calcutta and Hong Kong. When he passed away at age eighty-six at the Grand Hotel in Calcutta, a friend said, "He had come to the end of his great adventure. He was as close to heaven as if he had never left New York. He had been faithful."

The truth is that if you are being molded into the image of Christ every day, and if the Holy Spirit is doing His ongoing work in you, and if you are doing all that you can to serve God as the days and months and years are piled upon one another, then you're going to *shine*. Think of what the Spirit of God can do within someone who has lived half a century or more. Think of the fruit of the Spirit (see Galatians 5:22–23) continuing to blossom in your life. Think of that fruit coming into season as you reach your ripening years. Decline? Old age? We should call those years the *harvest* years, when the best, sweetest things in your life become ripe and delicious.

One of the most pervasive and cynical lies of our time is that all the good stuff comes in the first half of life—that after you reach sixty, it's all downhill. Bruce Larson summed up the challenge when he wrote these words:

> A life of safety is no life at all, whatever your vocation. Still, we are programmed from an early age to start providing for a safe and secure future. Through pension funds and retirement benefits, we work toward removing all risk from our lives by the time we are 65. Yet in the three societies sociologists have studied where people normally live to 100 and frequently to 120, there is no special treatment for the aged. . . . Scientists who have studied these societies have found they have nothing in common in terms of climate, diet, geography or lifestyle. But in all three places, the inhabitants are expected to live normal lives with no cushion for safety. They continue to work, tend fields and keep shops until they die at 100 plus. I am convinced that God never invented old age. Death is a gift, but old age is man's invention. It is a cultural blight in our lifetime.[6]

George Bernard Shaw, though lacking godly insight, came close to the essence of the man I want to be in these words:

> This is the true joy in life—being used for a purpose recognized by yourself as a mighty one, being a force of nature instead of a feverish, selfish little clod of ailments and grievances, complaining that the world will not devote itself to making you happy. . . . I want to be thoroughly used up when I die, for the harder I work, the more I live. I rejoice in life for its own sake. Life is no brief candle to me. It is sort of a splendid torch which I've got a hold of for the moment, and I want to make it burn as brightly as possible before handing it on to future generations.[7]

Caleb, J. Vernon McGee, Billy Graham, Cliff Barrows, George Beverly Shea, and so many others I could name have given out that lovely radiance of a seasoned life well lived. The candle flickers briefly into a glorious crown of flame before it expires. Don't even consider shutting down your life as you hit the years of culmination. Someone once said during a covered-dish dinner, just before the dessert was brought in, "Save your fork—the best is yet to come!"

Truly it is. When we dine, the final plate is the sweetest dish of all. Why should your life be any different? Follow God wholeheartedly, and make it so.

17

**LIFE
WIDE
OPEN**

UNLEASHING *the* POWER

of a PASSIONATE LIFE

Enjoy the Journey

HETTY GREEN HAD A SINGULAR PASSION: She wanted to be the richest woman on the face of the earth. The fire inside her burned intensely if not brightly, for it was a dark fire, and it eventually consumed her.

She lived at the beginning of the twentieth century, but she barely noticed the exciting times that were passing her by. Her wealth created an empire, but she had almost no friends or loved ones within that empire. She might have been beloved, influential, and celebrated—wide open for joy and fulfillment—but she locked herself within the prison of her obsession.

At the time of her death, Hetty Green's estate was valued at $95 million—quite an accomplishment for a woman in 1916. It is estimated that her fortune would be worth $17.3 billion today, and she is the only woman on a recent list of the forty richest Americans in history.

But where was the joy? When children saw Hetty Green coming in her long black dress, they fled, thinking she was a witch. Indeed, she was known in financial circles as "The Witch of Wall Street." With all her millions of dollars, she bought boxes of broken cookies in bulk to save money and dined on cold oatmeal to avoid the cost of heating it. Worst of all, her son was forced to have his leg amputated because she refused to pay for medical treatment that might have saved it.

When she died—characteristically in the course of an argument on the virtues of skim milk—Hetty Green was singularly miserable. She is perhaps the poster child for the dark side of passion, or, to be more accurate, *obsession*. For the kind of passion we've explored in this book could never make for such a dark and somber journey.

There is a happy ending of sorts: Hetty Green's children and grandchildren decided to make the world a better place with her fortune. They have given generously to hospitals, universities, the Girl Scouts, Christian charities, and libraries. The Web site for her trust now bears this message: "The Hetty Green Historical Society has recently received non-profit status—sorry, Hetty!"[1] These descendants have realized that the true profit is not measured by a balance sheet but by the joy it brings to the world.

Is this chapter about the evils of finance? Not at all. The real issue is what drives the passion inside us. We must be careful how we tend those flames, for if the motivations are ungodly ones, they will distort everything about us until the person who arrives at the destination is tragically unrecognizable from the one who departed.

True passion, godly passion, is lit by the sunshine of delight rather than the darkness of obsession. God wants us to enjoy the journey because He enjoys our enjoyment of it. I believe He might have said to Hetty Green, "If only you could have had the joy of your fortune that your children have enjoyed! If only you could have seen that you can gain the whole world and lose your soul. I own the cattle on a thousand hills, and My heart's delight is in sharing the bounty with My children. My daughter, you transformed the blessings of wealth to a poverty of the heart."

All of this is my way of saying to you, *Pursue your passion, but don't forget to have fun!* The kingdom of God is a celebration, not a sweatshop.

Certainly there will be struggles at work, conflicts in relationships, financial crises, doubts about God, and all the rest. The passionate life neither blinds you to the real world nor numbs you to its pain. Rather, as the fire of passion ignites within you, you will find the power to triumph over temptations, persevere through problems, and optimize opportunities. And at the end of the day, you'll sleep well, being content and fulfilled. Jesus says to you, "Come to Me, all you who labor and are heavy laden, and I will give you rest. Take My yoke upon you and learn from Me, for I am gentle and lowly in heart, and you will find rest for your souls. For My yoke is easy and My burden is light" (Matthew 11:28–30).

Rest for our soul, indeed—sometimes we lose that even in play. Have you noticed our propensity for making games into drudgery? Mark Twain said that golf is "a good walk spoiled." We start out enjoying the fine day, the smell of the fresh-cut grass, the beauty of the course. But the game itself can be frustrating to say the least. It seems so simple: Just hit the small white ball into the hole. But as every golfer knows, the challenge is to hit the ball accurately despite the infinite combination of body movements, club choices, swing speeds, ball locations, and weather conditions involved in every shot.

Golf is a competitive sport, but you're not really competing against the other players in your foursome. Ultimately you're competing against the golf course and against yourself. That's why golf is a sufficient challenge when played alone. For each course, a golf expert has determined that you should be able to play the entire eighteen holes in something in the vicinity of seventy-two strokes. That's called *par*. Every golfer competes against par, trying to beat it or to come as close as possible. And the golfer is always competing against himself—how he did last time, how he's done so far today, and how he'd like to do.

The golfer spends increasingly large sums of money on his equipment, desperately hoping to find any possible edge for his game, desperately hoping the problem is in the club and not the one who swings it. The golfer practices his swing in the playroom at home, in the backyard, at the office, and when no one is looking. He dreams eighteen holes at night.

Eventually he breaks one hundred, but there is no celebration—he is already fixated on breaking ninety. Once he gets there, he's already consumed by the number eighty. There's no end in sight.

There never has been, and never will be, a perfect round of golf. Bobby Jones, Jack Nicklaus, and even the phenomenal Tiger Woods have never played a perfect round. There have been perfect games pitched in baseball, perfect games bowled—but never a perfect game in golf, just an occasional hole in one. There are far too many variables for the entire game to be perfect, and the million-dollar golfer still has plenty of bad days.

Still, hundreds of thousands of golfers hit the fairways every day, pursuing perfection or at least a shot closer to it. The reason is that golf speaks to how God designed us. It's one way of getting in touch with the fire within that pushes us beyond our endurance toward improvement, toward achievement, toward perfection. Golf is passion pursued in the setting of God's beautiful green earth. And golf is for *smiles,* not for weeping, wailing, and gnashing of teeth.

Think of each day of your life as a round of golf. Some days are better than others. Some days you may finish near "par." Then there are the days when every shot goes into the sand trap, and you take the whole bag of clubs and hurl it into the lake—only to discover your car keys were in that bag. You sulk in your car on the way home, dripping wet, saying, "What's the use if I can never play the perfect game? Why even try?"

Because perfection is the goal, but it's not the journey. To live only for the goal is to live a life of terrible frustration. We'd better enjoy the trip, since we will never fully arrive. Passionate people know this. They understand what Paul, world traveler and champion of the faith, said: "Not that I have already attained, or am already perfected; but I press on!" (Philippians 3:12).

People of passion understand how it's possible to live the better part of a century and never quite reach your goal yet feel boundless joy and exhilaration. They understand the joy of the journey.

Take In the Beauty around You

Think of the obsessed golfer stalking through the golf course in pursuit of the god "par." He is intent on bringing a pure and holy sacrifice to the eighteenth hole. This golfer may be playing the green at Augusta, Georgia, or any of the greatest and most beautiful courses in the world. The sun is shining and the perfume of spring laces the air. The hills surrounding him are groomed and embellished to perfection. The waters dance, the birds sing, and the clouds are a canopy.

Yet he sees none of it, for he is pursuing "par."

Behind him comes another player, not an obsessed but a *passionate* golfer. He seems to be in no hurry at all. When he shoots, he is a study in concentration—though even then, there is a calm about him, a focus only achievable through a relaxed spirit. He exults in the sunshine and the sea of unbridled beauty around him. A chorus of praise swells up from his soul, as he is grateful just to be alive, to be a creature of God in this next-best thing to the Garden of Eden.

Passionate people stop and smell the roses, even when someone needs to take out the garbage. Passionate people see the work of God though it escapes the ordinary person's eye. Nothing beautiful, no matter how small or obscure, evades the glance of the one who lives the wide-open life. Passionate people see the best in all those around them and find a way of bringing out that best. They live in the wonder of worship, and they resonate with the words of this old German hymn:

> When morning gilds the skies my heart awaking cries:
> May Jesus Christ be praised!
> Alike at work and prayer, to Jesus I repair:
> May Jesus Christ be praised![2]

Explore the treasure in the crimson wings of a ladybug. Pause to close your eyes and welcome the caress of the breeze on your face.

Go to the woods and listen to the symphony of nature: the chorus of rustling leaves and creaking branches, the wind whistling like flute and piccolo, the solo of the songbird, the snare drum of clicking insects, and the timpani of a bullfrog.

It may take some time to loosen the fetters of an uptight week, but I know you can do it. Lose yourself in the wonder of God's artistry; fall in love with life all over again. Find out what touches you so deeply that tears well up in your eyes, and go ahead—let yourself get a little sloppy and sentimental just this once. I promise I won't tell a soul!

Ask God to open your eyes to the details around you, His hidden fingerprints on all that envelops you. This world is His handiwork, and it's more than a cold biological habitation for goal-driven laboratory specimens—it's a tour de force of divine artistry, and it's *your* palatial home. The Lord can't show you the mansion He has prepared for you in the next world—you wouldn't survive the shock of its beauty—but the majestic Alps, the exotic Amazon River, and the fruited plains of America are just a foretaste of what He has prepared for us in our eternal home. Stop and think about that.

Stop and think also about the journey of your life, just as beautiful, just as entrancing, and also a foretaste of the heavenly life that awaits you. This passionate journey toward perfection, though the goal will never be reached in this life, is of divine itinerary. It is a journey laid out for you, and only you, at the dawn of creation. It is as distinctly designed for you as your fingerprints. Every high vista and every challenging valley is part of the tour laid out by God, a journey of transformation that will make you resemble Christ a little more each day.

So much to live; so much to give:

> To touch the cup with eager lips and taste, not drain it;
> To woo and tempt and court a bliss—and not attain it;
> To fondle and caress a joy, yet hold it lightly,
> Lest it become necessity and cling too tightly;

To watch the sun set in the west without regretting;
To hail its advent in the east—the night forgetting;
To smother care in happiness and grief in laughter;
To hold the present close—not questioning hereafter;
To have enough to share—to know the joy of giving;
To thrill with all the sweets of life—this is living.

Let a fountain of gratitude well up from your soul, and let the waters of that gratitude drench every part of your being. Gratitude is the true fountain of youth, and its essence is joy in humility.

NEVER STOP LEARNING ABOUT LIFE

For passionate people, the whole world is a university. They understand that formal schooling was just a way of learning to learn; real education comes in the journey of living. These people are askers of questions and readers of books in all manner of topics. They seek learning not as a discipline but a joy. What is life like in this country? What was our history during that particular era? How does this form of technology work? What are the newest and most innovative ways to accomplish this mission?

Passionate people don't identify themselves as salesmen, housewives, doctors, clerks, or even husbands, wives, or parents. They are proud of those designations, but they see themselves in less restrictive terms. If you call yourself a salesman enough times, then eventually you're going to be transformed to the image of a salesman. If you identify yourself only as a housewife, that's the sole identify you'll determine for yourself. Passionate people see themselves as complex, multidimensional children of God. They see themselves as workers, players, lovers, artists, craftsmen, travelers, and celebrators. They define themselves in verbs rather than nouns. They speak the dialect of challenge and adventure. Look into their eyes, and you'll see the reflection of distant horizons.

Walk into a university classroom, and you'll see a passionate grandmother, studying a foreign language so she can share Christ on her short-term mission trip to Guatemala. Visit a health spa, and you'll find a passionate paraplegic, pushing the boundaries of what medical science says he is capable of doing with his life. Go to any library, and you'll find passionate people consuming knowledge and expanding the borders of their life. Almost anywhere you go, look for the challengers and adventurers who may not be the most gifted or intelligent or athletic—but they're the ones whose fires burn so brightly that you're likely to catch the stray spark. After you leave that person's presence, you'll feel that you're somehow better, more thoughtful, more awake and in tune than you were before.

I don't mean to imply that passionate people live some kind of utopian dream with all the time they need and the financial freedom to pursue every whim. Not at all. These people are master pruners, knowing what to cut out of their life, making yes choices and no choices almost on a momentary basis. Passionate people watch less and less television. They revere the sanctity of time. And they're willing to make the hard choices that make their life more fruitful.

Passionate people never try to slide by with a passing grade, take a shortcut, or give minimal effort. They care less for grades than learning, less for the destination than the journey. They care less for how they appear than how they grow. And above all, they will do what it takes, pay any price, and travel any distance to grow.

And of course, passionate people go deeper and deeper with God, becoming more intimate with prayer and more intense with Bible study. They spend more time alone with Him and more time elsewhere with the vital sense of His presence. They understand that all too few people have gone as deep with God as it is possible to delve. His presence is the true final frontier, and there is so much unexplored territory. They want to push out to the horizon where just a handful have gone—maybe a step further, who knows? Passionate people want to find out just how near to the throne it is possible to draw in this earthly life.

Yes, passionate people are difficult to quantify because they are always changing, always transforming, always between where they were yesterday and where they plan to be tomorrow. Passionate people don't make their home in the status quo but push forward to new ways and new possibilities.

TAKE LAUGHTER SERIOUSLY

To come full circle, let me say it again—don't forget to have fun. Here is the delightful truth: Passionate people like to laugh. Leave the black dresses and cold breakfasts to the Hetty Greens of the world. Passionate people aren't those souls who are so earnest, so holy, that you would rather keep your distance. On the contrary, they love a good joke.

Wise King Solomon wrote, "A cheerful disposition is good for your health; gloom and doom leave you bone-tired" (Proverbs 17:22 MSG). Why do passionate people tend to have a good sense of humor? Because humor is basically perspective; it is the ability to stand apart from life and see ourselves and this world as they truly are. It is the ability to see the sharp contrasts and odd juxtapositions that are the raw material of humor. The obsessed golfer and the preoccupied stockbroker are the ones who never smile. They lack that perspective because their life has become narrowed to the bitter obsession that drives them.

Not so for passionate people. They have 20–20 vision, telescopic and microscopic so that they see the fine point and the distant star. The more they see, the better perspective they have, and the more they realize that this life is short and is to be lived joyfully. The little things and possessions and causes we pursue are here for a moment before they become vapor, but we humans are eternal creatures, made to resemble God Himself. To realize that is to feel joy. To realize that is to feel a smile creeping across our face, and to find ourselves laughing.

Passionate people outwork, outplay, outlearn, outlaugh,

outlove, and *outlive* everyone else—and somehow they have more fun doing it!

Are we having fun yet? Don't laugh—it may be the best test of whether you're living the passionate life, the soulful life, the life wide open.

LIFE WIDE OPEN

UNLEASHING *the* POWER *of a* PASSIONATE LIFE

Epilogue: The Promise of the Passionate Life

W E ' V E   F O U N D   I T : the treasure we've sought together through these chapters, this study of scriptural gems, and these moments of reflection concerning our hopes and dreams. I can't hope to have covered every conceivable issue that you'll face in your journey to the life wide open, but it is my hope and prayer that all the basics, all the key themes, and all the ammunition you need have been provided to you.

Now that you've unlocked the secrets and discovered where the treasure lies, will you go after it? There still remains that one step, my friend. I've known people who study the pursuit of God for a lifetime yet never leave for the quest. Imagine spending your life becoming an expert on automobiles without ever once riding in one. All the books in the world would not convey to you the experience of being at the wheel of a fine convertible with the top down, feeling the wind in your hair as you cruised down the freeway on a summer day.

The life wide open, too, demands to be *lived* rather than studied. Would a Rand-McNally map of the island of Oahu give you any idea of the beauty of that island? Not at all. Similarly, this book is the road map to a life wide open, but it's time for you to begin the authentic experience. Your quest is launched today, and it centers in

197

your relationship with the Lord, who has summoned you for the journey. In the end, your passion will be for *Him*. The ultimate thrill is seeing the curtains open, inch by inch, to reveal a bit more about the awesome God you've only seen in a mirror dimly.

As a longtime traveler on the road of passion, I'm excited to know a new pilgrim is on the road to glory. In a way, I envy you for those thrilling moments of discovery when you experience new facets of our Lord's love and tenderness for the first time. However, I can tell you that the journey only gets richer, deeper, and more beautiful.

Remember, you are a citizen of heaven—an ambassador from another world—gradually becoming more aware of the startling truth of your kingdom identity. In this darkened world you are a foreigner and an alien, just as the Scriptures say, but you are bound for your true home. As you travel each mile of this homeward course, you will realize all the more that this is your heart, this is your passion, and this is where you truly belong. And after a taste of the wide-open life on the wide-open road toward the Savior, you will never, never want to go back.

My friend, let me leave you with this final challenge: Be passionate about every portion of your life. Nothing is more death-like than the life unlived. Dare to live; dare to meet the day with all that your soul can offer it.

I deeply want to avoid dying before I have truly lived. I want to be a pioneer who pushes further and further into that last frontier—the transforming presence and power of God.

I want people to say of me, "This was a person of passion."

I want them to say, "This was a person of peace."

I want them to know that I met each moment and each decision and each relationship with all my heart, mind, and soul—and that I explored every new vista God presented for me to explore. I want other people to be driven to the passionate pursuit of God simply from knowing me—for above all, I want to glorify God and enjoy Him forever.

Epilogue: The Promise of the Passionate Life

What about you, my friend? Where to from here? As I close my eyes, I can summon a mental picture of you, closing this book as if rolling up the old treasure map. There is a glint of adventure in your eye—the spark of a faraway fire, of a kingdom that calls you. I see your squared shoulders, your foot restless to take that first step forward, and I know you're setting out on the ultimate journey, the adventure every one of us was created to share.

I know you're serious about this quest. You might just catch up with some of the rest of us travelers and even leave us behind in the passion of your quest—to which we'll laugh for sheer joy and turn our heels toward the horizon to catch up with you.

Godspeed!

Notes

INTRODUCTION: OPEN WIDE!

1. Glenn Van Ekeren, ed., *Speaker's Sourcebook II: Quotes, Stories & Anecdotes for Every Occasion* (Englewood Cliffs, N.J.: Prentice Hall, 1994), 190.

CHAPTER 1: PEDAL-TO-THE-METAL LIVING

1. Ed. Irving Shepard, *Jack London's Tale of Adventure* (New York: Doubleday, 1956), vii.

CHAPTER 2: GIVE EVERYTHING YOUR ALL

1. Lance Armstrong with Sally Jenkins, *It's Not About the Bike* (New York: G. P. Putnam's Sons, 2000), 1.

2. Eugene Robinson, *It Takes Endurance* (Sisters, Ore.: Multnomah, 1998), 25–26; quoted in Mike Nappa, *The Courage to Be Christian* (West Monroe, La.: Howard, 2001), 1–3.

3. Bud Paxon, *Threading the Needle* (New York: Harper Collins, 1998), 28.

4. Summarized from Rick Warren, *The Purpose-Driven Life* (Grand Rapids: Zondervan, 2002).

5. Frederick Buechner, *Wishful Thinking: A Theological ABC* (San Francisco: HarperSanFrancisco, 1993).

CHAPTER 3: YOU GOTTA HAVE HEART

1. Mike Nappa, *The Courage to Be Christian* (West Monroe, La.: Howard, 2001), 1–3.

CHAPTER 4: WHO'S IT ALL FOR?

1. Jack Welch with John A. Byrne, *Jack, Straight from the Gut* (New York: Warner, 2001), 385.
2. Kenneth Caugel, quoted in Max Anders, gen. ed., *Holman New Testament Commentary* (Nashville: Broadman & Holman, 1998), 256.
3. Brother Lawrence, *The Practice of the Presence of God* (Westwood, N.J.: Fleming H. Revell, 1958), 6.
4. Ibid.
5. Bill McCartney, sermon at Shadow Mountain Community Church, El Cajon, California, 26 January 2003.

CHAPTER 5: DRAW DEEPLY FROM THE WELL WITHIN

1. Jim Collins, *Good to Great* (New York: HarperCollins, 2001), 109.
2. Og Mandino, *The Greatest Salesman in the World* (New York: Bantam Books, 1983).
3. Erwin Raphael McManus, *Uprising—A Revolution of the Soul* (Nashville: Thomas Nelson, 2003), 24.
4. A. T. Pierson, quoted in J. Oswald Sanders, *The Holy Spirit and His Gifts* (Grand Rapids: Zondervan, 1970), 115.

Notes

CHAPTER 6: A FORK IN THE ROAD

1. "I Have Decided to Follow Jesus," composer unknown.
2. Rosa Parks, *Quiet Strength* (Grand Rapids, MI: Zondervan, 1995, 2000).
3. Michael Card, "Wounded in the House of Friends," *Virtue* (March/April 1991), 28–29.

CHAPTER 8: WHEN THE FIRE GOES OUT

1. http://www.surfline.com for biographical info; sermon by Bruce Theilemann, "Legions of the Unjazzed," which can be found at http://www.preachingtoday.com.
2. Source unknown.
3. Sue Monk Kidd, *When the Heart Waits* (San Francisco: HarperCollins, 1990), 71.

CHAPTER 10: ME? NO WAY!

1. Leighton Ford, *Good News is for Sharing* (Colorado Springs: David C. Cook, 1977), 67.
2. Adapted from Josh McDowell, *See Yourself as God Sees You* (Wheaton, Ill.: Tyndale, 1999), 100–101.

CHAPTER 11: LAND OF THE GIANTS

1. Paul Tillich, "An Ontology of Anxiety," *The Courage to Be* (Yale University Press, 1952).
2. Susan Sontag, quoted in *Time Out* [London], 19 August 1992.
3. Lewis B. Smedes, *Shame and Grace: Healing the Shame We Don't Deserve* (New York: Harper, 1993), chapter 2.
4. Erwin Raphael McManus, *Uprising—A Revolution of the Soul* (Nashville: Thomas Nelson, 2003), 38.

LIFE WIDE OPEN

CHAPTER 12: SOAR ABOVE YOUR CIRCUMSTANCES

1. Bill Russell and Taylor Branch, *Second Wind: The Memoirs of an Opinionated Man* (New York: Random House, 1979).

CHAPTER 13: REMEMBER WHAT IT'S ALL ABOUT

1. Augustine, *Confessions* 10.27.
2. J. C. Ryle, *Practical Religion* (London: James Clarke & Co., Ltd., 1959), 130.
3. "God Be in My Heart," Sarum Primer, 1538.

CHAPTER 14: IGNITING A PASSION FOR GOD

1. Howard Taylor, *Hudson Taylor's Spiritual Secret* (Chicago: Moody, 1979), 21.
2. A. W. Tozer, *The Pursuit of God* (Harrisburg, Penn.: Christian Publishing, 1948), 17.
3. Ibid., 66–67.
4. *Eternity Magazine,* August 1966; quoted by John MacArthur, *Kingdom Living Here and Now* (Chicago: Moody, 1980), 92–93.
5. Martyn Lloyd-Jones, *Studies in the Sermon on the Mount* (Grand Rapids: Eerdmans, 1959), 173–74.
6. Sherwood Eliot Wirt, *A Thirst for God: Reflections on the Forty-second and Forty-third Psalms* (Grand Rapids: Zondervan, 1980), 25.

CHAPTER 15: KEEP THE FIRE BURNING

1. Calvin Miller, *Into the Depths of God* (Minneapolis, Minn: Bethany House, 2000), 227.
2. Herbert S. Long, "Foreword"; quoted in Eric Liddell, *The Disciplines of the Christian Life* (Nashville: Abingdon, 1983), 13–18.

3. Ibid., 18.

CHAPTER 16: WIDE OPEN ALL THE WAY

1. Anna Wilde Matthews, "Eternally Popular, This Radio Preacher Actually Died in 1988," *Wall Street Journal,* 19 December 2002, A1.

2. Lee Eisenberg, "Taking the Long, Sharp View," *Esquire,* 100, no. 6 (1983): 305.

3. Peter M. Senge, *The Fifth Discipline: The Art & Practice of the Learning Organization* (New York: Doubleday, 1990), 7–8.

4. Ibid., 147.

5. Calvin Miller, *Into the Depths of God* (Minneapolis, Minn: Bethany House, 2000), 226.

6. Bruce Larson, *There's a Lot More to Health Than Not Being Sick* (Waco, Tex.: Word, 1981), 75–76.

7. George Bernard Shaw, *Man and Superman* (New York: Penguin, 1950), preface.

CHAPTER 17: ENJOY THE JOURNEY

1. From the Virtual Vermont Web Site, which can be found at: www.virtualvermont.com/history/hgreen; also the Hetty Green Historical Society at: www.hettygreen.com.

2. "When Morning Gilds the Skies," tr. Edward Caswall (1814–1878).